175+
Things to Do
BEFORE
YOU
GRADUATE
COLLEGE

D0089877

175+

Things to Do
BEFORE YOU GRADUATE COLLEGE

YOUR BUCKET LIST FOR THE ULTIMATE COLLEGE EXPERIENCE!

☑ Create a Dorm Scavenger Hunt

☑ Try Every Item on the Dining Hall Menu

☑ Strike a Pose with Your School Mascot

☑ Visit a Museum for FREE with Your Student ID

☑ Go Out for an Epic Brunch

CHARLOTTE LAKE

Adams Media
New York   London   Toronto   Sydney   New Delhi

Adams Media

An Imprint of Simon & Schuster, Inc.

57 Littlefield Street

Avon, Massachusetts 02322

Copyright © 2021 by Simon & Schuster, Inc.

All rights reserved, including the right to reproduce this book or portions thereof in any form whatsoever. For information address Adams Media Subsidiary Rights Department, 1230 Avenue of the Americas, New York, NY 10020.

First Adams Media trade paperback edition April 2021

ADAMS MEDIA and colophon are trademarks of Simon & Schuster.

For information about special discounts for bulk purchases, please contact Simon & Schuster Special Sales at 1-866-506-1949 or business@simonandschuster.com.

The Simon & Schuster Speakers Bureau can bring authors to your live event. For more information or to book an event contact the Simon & Schuster Speakers Bureau at 1-866-248-3049 or visit our website at www.simonspeakers.com.

Interior design by Michelle Kelly

Interior images by Alaya Howard; © 123RF, Getty Images

Manufactured in the United States of America

1 2021

Library of Congress Cataloging-in-Publication Data has been applied for.

ISBN 978-1-5072-1542-5

ISBN 978-1-5072-1543-2 (ebook)

Many of the designations used by manufacturers and sellers to distinguish their products are claimed as trademarks. Where those designations appear in this book and Simon & Schuster, Inc., was aware of a trademark claim, the designations have been printed with initial capital letters.

Dedication

To my parents,
For raising me to believe the world is my oyster and
always supporting my dreams of world domination.

Contents

CHAPTER 4: ROUNDING OUT ACADEMICS 109

For Bryn

★ Buy a fuller journal

Introduction

College: It's an amazing time where you experience an unparalleled amount of opportunities, possibilities, and new adventures. But there's also a lot of pressure to make these years the best of your life *and* somehow set yourself up for a happy and successful future once you graduate. How do you figure out what career path fits your interests? Or where to find friends who will cheer you on and encourage you to be your best self? And what activities will build you up and inspire your dreams?

It might feel like a lot to take on, but luckily, that's where this book comes in! Instead of feeling overwhelmed by the pressure to do college "right," *175+ Things to Do Before You Graduate College* will help you figure out what's important to *you* and how to make the most of these pivotal years. Here, you'll find more than 175 activities that will bring fun *and* success to your college years, including:

- Getting to know all the buildings better with a game of hide-and-seek
- Saying yes to every social invite for a week
- Developing a mentor relationship with an upperclassman
- Sitting in on free guest talks
- Becoming a teaching assistant for a favorite class

Whether you're just entering your freshman year or are getting ready to rock senior year, commuting from home or living on (or off) campus, you'll discover unique ideas that will help you have a happy and rewarding experience at college. Flip through to the activities that stand out to you, and use the pages at the end of each chapter to create your own personalized bucket list items for each major aspect of college life. Remember, it's all about what matters to *you*, so you can change, tweak, and update your list throughout your experiences.

College is not a task to complete; it's an opportunity to learn, grow, and have fun. It's time to start taking advantage of everything it has to offer!

How to Use This Book

From visiting the Grand Canyon to falling in love, everyone has things they want to do, see, and experience at some point in their life. The sum of all these personal goals is what's known as a bucket list. A college bucket list is essentially the same concept, but focuses on the years you spend studying for your undergraduate degree. Your college bucket list includes everything you hope to accomplish before you graduate.

The first things that come to your mind when you think "bucket list" are probably the big-ticket items. You know—semesters abroad in exotic locations, thrill-seeking adventures off campus—things like that. But the truth is that there's no strict set of standards for what deserves a spot on a bucket list. It's actually very open to interpretation! Your college bucket list can include those larger goals like finishing a 5k or landing your dream internship, as well as little things like seeing your favorite band in concert, or tailgating at a football game—and everything in between. The common thread among them is simply that they're meaningful to *you*.

WHY SHOULD I HAVE A COLLEGE BUCKET LIST?

As a college student, you're one busy bee. With classes to attend, assignments to complete, social events to go to, and friends to see, your daily to-do list can feel never-ending! Even for those with an excellent memory, it's nearly impossible for your brain to keep track of everything on its own. The same goes for goals and aspirations. It isn't a stretch to realize that when you're preoccupied with the hustle and bustle of college life, some (if not most) of the things you want to do or see are bound to slip your mind.

Creating a bucket list, either as a physical list on paper or a list on your phone or computer, will help keep it all fresh in your mind, and you'll be able to visually track your progress. Who doesn't love the satisfaction of checking things off a to-do list? Simply moving your aspirations out of your mind and into the physical plane of existence can jump-start you into action! Plus, having a list can help you accomplish goals that are more time-sensitive (like submitting your paperwork to graduate). It's a lot easier to avoid accidentally missing out on an opportunity when you've already taken steps to plan ahead.

Creating a college bucket list is also crucial because it's a thought-provoking task in itself. It opens up the space for self-reflection and encourages you to do some soul-searching. Figuring out what is most important to you is the first step in making the most of your college experience.

THE KEYS TO A GOOD COLLEGE BUCKET LIST

But what *are* the most important things to you? It can be hard to know what really matters, or what might seem like a big deal now, but will likely be forgotten about a few years down the line. However, thinking in terms of different categories like academics, off-campus experiences, and friendships helps make it easier. When it comes to college bucket lists, there are seven main topics every good list addresses:

1. Maximizing your dorm-life experiences
2. Exploring on-campus activities beyond academics
3. Capitalizing on all the off-campus experiences calling your name

4. Pursuing academic opportunities that inspire and bolster your studies *and* future career goals

5. Creating your best self through self-care, healthy challenges, and more

6. Cultivating good karma by embracing the power of kindness

7. Taking advantage of last hurrahs before graduation

Each of the chapters in this book tackles one of these key topics, offering over a dozen unique, easy ways to live your college life to the fullest *and* prepare for what lies beyond these next few years.

SO HOW DO I CREATE MY OWN BUCKET LIST?

Each of the seven main elements for a good college bucket list opens a world of possibilities—and that's where your unique wants and needs come in to make a list personalized to you. Just like people, no two college bucket lists are exactly the same!

You can try out each activity in the following chapters to figure out what feels right or look through for activities that stand out. You can also use these activities as a jumping-off point to come up with brand-new ideas that are tailor-made to you and your college experiences. Challenge a friend to create a college bucket list at the same time so you can feed off of each other's ideas and encourage each other to check off each item before graduation day.

From lofty ambitions to everyday victories and young adulthood milestones, no personal ambition is too big or small to add to your list. Be sure to use the journal pages at the end of each chapter to keep track of your bucket list items for that category.

NEXT STEPS

Now that you've explored the reasons for creating a college bucket list and what elements make for a good list, you're ready to dive into the following activities—almost. Before you do, it's important to keep in mind that creating a well-rounded college bucket list is an on-going project. Don't feel like you need to decide everything you want to do right away! During your time at college, your perspective will likely shift and you may discover newfound importance in different areas of your life.

Also remember that this book is here as a guide, not an end-all, be-all of what you must do during college. You can tailor different activities to your specific wants and needs or follow them to a T—whatever feels right. You may also find yourself inspired by something you witness or hear about along the way. Be sure to jot down a quick note whenever this happens so you remember to add it to your own list later.

So, are you ready to make your college years the happiest and most successful they can be? Let's get started!

CHAPTER 1

Thriving (Not Just Surviving) in the Dorms

Looking back through the history of the word "dorm," you'll find it comes from the Latin word *dormitorium*, which literally means "sleeping place." Getting enough sleep is a huge part of thriving at college, but as far as dorm life goes, it's just the tip of the iceberg. Outside of classes, clubs, and special events, residence halls are the mingling hub for students living on campus. With close quarters, shared everything, open-door policies, and an endless stream of mixers, the opportunities to socialize are never-ending. Learning how to socialize and navigate new situations is an important part of your college experience. These skills will come in handy in all areas of your life, both now and after you've graduated.

Of course, even for the most extroverted extrovert, all of this socializing, sharing, and the pressure to do it all can get to be a little *much*. It's perfectly normal to feel overwhelmed at times. Luckily, this chapter provides a mix of activities you can do with others, as well as things to do solo, to help you get out of your comfort zone, be proactive about creating friendships, find different ways to enjoy solitude, and feel at ease in your surroundings.

Challenge Yourself to Learn One Fact about Everyone in Your Hall

The other students in your hall are the ones you'll have a chance to get to know better than anyone else because you'll essentially be living with them for an entire year. Keep your dorm room door open when you're not busy to encourage people to pop in to say hello. It's a guaranteed way to meet new people—without even trying.

You should also take a more active approach, however. And what better way to do so than a fun challenge? Make a point to introduce yourself to everyone in your hall and learn one fact about each person. (You can also keep track of who you've talked to and what you've learned in your phone or a notebook.)

Get started by simply walking the hall looking for open doors and stopping to chat with the people inside. It might feel awkward at first, but you'll get more comfortable over time, and it may even become a habit. Some students may be more reclusive because they're having a hard time adjusting or are struggling with homesickness. You can help them come out of their shell by simply engaging with them regularly (even just to say hello) and by inviting them to eat lunch and attend social events with you.

Over these small but frequent interactions, you're likely to become good friends with at least a few students in your hall. You'll also set a great example to the other students in fostering a sense of community among the dorms. You can promote even more bonding by challenging your new roommate(s) to do the same and seeing how your facts compare!

Find the Best Bathroom—the One Nobody Knows About

Most college bathrooms are less than pristine thanks to the constant stream of students filtering in and out all day long. The messes left behind and lack of privacy from door gaps make it challenging to find a moment of peace between your classes.

But beyond the heavily trafficked areas, there are usually cleaner, *calmer* restrooms waiting to be found. There's a certain joy to having your own private porcelain sanctuary in the eye of the storm. So, when you stumble upon that perfect bathroom (the one that even the staff doesn't seem to know exists), don't tell a soul. It'll be your little secret.

Create Your Own Dorm Oasis

College can be a difficult transition because of all the new surroundings, classes, and people. It's totally normal to experience some homesickness and need time alone to decompress. Even as you get further along in your college experience, you will still have those moments or even days where you just need to get away from constant socializing and activity. Having a place where you can retreat and recharge can make all the difference.

With fluorescent lighting and bare white walls, dorm rooms don't exactly scream "home." Thankfully, just a few decorative additions can turn your room into a much cozier space. And you don't need to go for broke to achieve the perfect look either!

For one thing, you can't go wrong with string lights. A couple of lamps or an LED light strip will work too—*anything* is better than the harsh overhead lighting. Flower and vine garlands are another easy way to give the whole room a less sterile feel. And of course, posters, tapestries, and framed photos of family members, pets, and hometown friends are classic staples for any dorm.

You can further express your unique style with temporary wallpaper, your own art, elements of your favorite hobbies, and more. Find inspiration online by browsing *Pinterest* for pictures of fully decorated dorms and easy DIYs. Just be sure to hang any decor with 3M Command strips and hooks to avoid damaging the walls (which could cost you part of your deposit)!

Build a Floor-Wide Blanket Fort

Students are encouraged to live on campus for at least their first year of college because it's the best way to expand your social circle. As a result, the dorms are an epicenter of activity.

On a Friday or weekend night, get to know your floor neighbors a little better by organizing a collaborative blanket fort. The bonding and fun will be through the roof no matter how successful or unsuccessful your venture might be. It'll be one of those nights you can look back on fondly for years to come.

Become the Laundry Room Guru

If you wear sweats or pajamas to class for a week straight, it's likely that no one will bat an eye. Most of your classmates are too preoccupied with their own thoughts to care about your fashion choices. Plus, many of them are probably rocking sweats or pajamas of their own. Pungent body odors, on the other hand, *will* attract negative attention.

Laundry is an inescapable chore, but nailing down a routine that is as painless as possible will minimize the hassle. To accomplish this, you should do your laundry once a week, instead of letting dirty clothes pile up for weeks on end. One load of laundry doesn't take long to complete. Dealing with an entire mountain of laundry, on the other hand, can easily eat up an entire day. You should also do your laundry when the laundry room is least busy so you don't have to fight for machines. The best time for laundry is usually on Friday and Saturday evenings, but pop into the laundry room on different days and at varying times to find out for sure. Not having to wait for someone to finally move their clothes out of the dryer will save you time and extra trips to and from the machines.

A drying rack can also reduce the amount of time you spend running back and forth to the laundry room. Most fabrics only take a few hours to dry. There are folding, as well as over-the-door options that won't take up much space in your dorm room. Air-drying will save you money and may even extend the life of your clothes!

Organize a
Board Game Night

If you think board games are boring, then you've been missing out! There are so many different types of games, and it seems like there are new ones coming out every year. A regular game night (weekly or at least monthly) can help you relieve stress while making connections with other students and trying something new.

Invite a few friends and have everyone bring a plus-one to expand your social group. You can even make it a hall-wide event by posting an invite for everyone to see. Try board games, card games, or even form a *Dungeons & Dragons* group! Take turns choosing the game to keep things fresh and interesting.

Talk to Your Roommate(s) about Expectations and Boundaries

In an ideal world, you and your college roommate(s) would become friends the instant you lock eyes. Alas, an equivalent to the Match.com algorithm isn't used to make room assignments. But don't let it rub you the wrong way if you end up being less than BFFs: It can still work (and work well) even if you don't hit it off right away! Getting along with your roommate(s) will make your living space feel more comfortable and help the time go by a lot better than gritting your teeth through the experience.

Once you are moved into your dorm, sit down with your roommate(s) and discuss how each of you feels about guests, organization, noise, and other preferences. Yes, even if you are living with friends, it's still important to have this discussion! A small miscommunication can easily snowball into a much bigger problem and cause real tension in your friendship. Talking it out, on the other hand, can actually strengthen your relationship.

Discussing boundaries will help you set clear expectations for one another and your shared space so you can avoid possible issues down the road. There will likely be some changes during the school year, so be sure to communicate frequently and honestly to avoid building up feelings of resentment.

Keep your area tidy, be aware of your noise level, and find at least one thing in common with your roommate(s) if you aren't already friends. You don't have to be best friends with every person you live with, but you do need to respect them and their things. Most people will respond positively to you treating them respectfully. And if a situation does get out of hand, ask your resident assistant for help with finding a solution.

Create a Dorm Scavenger Hunt

Scavenger hunts are a great way to blow off steam, make fun memories, and get closer to your roommate(s) or other students in your resident hall. When you're brainstorming ideas, get creative and be as specific as possible. Include items to find, like:

- A water bottle with a school sticker
- Pizza coupons
- Someone sleeping in a common area
- Someone wearing a Greek life shirt
- Anything unique to your dorm

It can be a fun activity to do with just your friends, the entire floor, or anyone in your hall who wants to join in!

Do Tarot Card Readings under a Full Moon

Whether or not you believe in witches, magic, or otherworldly creatures, the lore behind tarot is fascinating. There's even a belief that you shouldn't buy your first tarot card deck: It should be gifted to you by someone else. If you want to keep to this tradition, you can ask a friend to buy you one and return the favor. But this rule is not set in stone, so don't hesitate to buy a deck for yourself if you want to! Look online or check out a metaphysical supply store to find a tarot deck with an art style you love.

When it's time for a reading, really channel those mystical vibes by gathering a small group of friends, your roommate(s), or some students from your dorm hall, under the light of a full moon. Bonus points if it's Friday the thirteenth, or on/during the week of Halloween when everyone is wearing a costume. The middle of any sports field on campus is a perfect setting. Sit in a circle, and take turns being the card reader. Your deck may come with instructions for how to read the cards, or you can find easy tutorials and card information on your smartphone to help you.

This activity is sure to bring you and your companions closer together—no matter what the cards reveal about your future.

Bring the Holidays to Your Dorm with Hilarious Holiday Cards

You know those old pictures of your parents or grandparents in which they thought they looked really cool but now can't help but laugh at themselves? That's the look you're going for here. Most holiday cards are forgotten as soon as they're removed from the fridge. But not this year!

Creating a funny card is a great project to help you bond with your roommate(s) or other students in your hall and get into the holiday spirit—especially if it's your first time spending part or all of the holiday away from home. You can set up a common room, put your heads together to brainstorm creative ideas, and fuel your creation with plenty of snacks.

For a memorable photo shoot:

- Throw it back to the trends of yesteryear: Try outfits and hairstyles inspired by a past decade like the eighties or nineties.
- Consider making your childhood pet(s) the focal point: Start with a photo you already have on your phone, and use an editing app to make them appear more festive.
- Make use of graphic design skills to superimpose your faces on a funny background.

For more ideas, look online for easy tutorials and search "awkward holiday card" for inspiration. The more perfectly imperfect your card is, the better: Imperfections only add to the humor!

Say Yes to Every Social Activity for a Week

Saying yes to any invitations and opportunities that come along is a great way to put yourself out there, especially during freshman week or student orientation! There will be a lot of "icebreaker" activities that may not seem like your cup of tea, but instead of opting out, try going with the flow and see what happens. As you loosen up a bit you'll start to feel less awkward (everyone else looks just as silly, after all) and have some fun.

If nothing else, you're sure to meet loads of new people, which will help smooth over your transition to college life and make each school experience that much better. Most other students are just as eager to make friends. Seeing one familiar face in each of your classes will make all the difference between feeling completely alone and feeling like you've got this.

Go All Out with Your Costume for Halloween

If you thought Halloween was fun as a kid, just wait until you experience it at college. Some schools have wacky traditions to celebrate the day, but the main event is going out and mingling with other students. Halloween transforms into Halloweekend: Instead of limiting the festivities to just one day, there are two or three days' worth of celebrations.

As you get older, there are less chances to dress up and go all out for Halloween, so wear that costume (or costumes) you've always dreamed of! Check out social media for ideas, as well as *Pinterest* for cool and easy DIY costume tutorials. You can save money by assembling your costume with thrifted pieces instead of buying a premade outfit. And if you're a little unsure, you can make it a group costume with your roommate(s) or other friends. Group costumes are awesome to put together and a blast to wear.

Take an Outdoor Nap

College can be a lot of hustle and bustle, but you'll never regret taking time to enjoy the simpler things in life. The first day of nice weather after the colder months is just as momentous an event on campus as any holiday.

Compared to your average nap in the dorm room, there's just something more refreshing about taking a siesta outside. Waking up with the sun on your face leaves you with a peaceful feeling—and a boost in vitamin D. Ultimately, a little relaxation goes a long way in your mood and mindset, so pull out a big blanket, tie up a hammock, or nestle into the grass for a snooze.

Join an Intramural Team for a Sport You've Never Played

Intramurals are casual sports for students of all activity and skill levels. Playing on an intramural team is a fantastic way to try a sport you haven't played before, get some exercise, bond with other students, and take your mind off of school for a while.

Many colleges offer tons of different—and sometimes unexpected—sports to sign up for, from Quidditch and table tennis to rugby and ultimate Frisbee. And it doesn't matter if you're not a pro! It can actually be more fun to try something outside of your comfort zone because you'll get to watch yourself improve over the season.

Intramurals are popular, so sign up early to make sure you get a spot on a team. Also remember that winning isn't everything—although the champion T-shirts can be pretty sweet! If you do get really into it, a leadership position will look good on your resume too.

Put Together a Time Capsule

It's surprising how much you can change in a few years—or even just from one year to the next. As each year ends and another begins, you'll likely be different, but you may not realize just how different and in exactly what ways.

A time capsule is a fun gift for your future self that will help you remember who you were, whether one year ago or from freshman year to graduation day, and appreciate who you've become. Here are some ideas for what to include in your time capsule:

- **A letter to yourself.** You could include the goals and dreams you're working toward, what you're obsessed with at the moment, or a raw, diary-type entry about your current life situation.

- **A letter from someone else.** Ask a parent, grandparent, or good friend to write a letter to your future self. What they include is up to them—and a great surprise for you.

- **Meaningful pictures.** Include favorite snapshots of your childhood pet, family members, or you and your BFF. You can even take a picture of yourself the day of to toss in!

- **A CD or flash drive.** Upload your favorite songs to listen to when you open the capsule.

- **Other small items with special meaning.** Party decorations from your last birthday, a poem you wrote, an art project you're proud of, or concert ticket stubs may be some of your prized possessions.

The beauty of a time capsule is that there's no wrong way to make one. There are many more things you might want to include, so think outside of the box. Once you have everything ready, put it all in the container of your choice (a coffee tin or shoebox is easy to come by). Choose the date you want to open it on and write it on the top of the container. There's no need to bury the time capsule, but if you do, just make sure you have some way to remember where it is! Otherwise, keep it safe by sending it to your parents' house or leaving it tucked away in the back of your closet.

Be Proactive about Safe Sex

Maybe you're not planning on having sex anytime soon, but the fact of the matter is there's a possibility that you will be sexually active at some point during college. And the last thing you want is to be hot and heavy in the moment, realize you don't have protection, and either have to stop the fun or throw caution to the wind. Think about it like this: You're more likely to make smart decisions about sex if you're prepared.

And being prepared is easy! Take advantage of the free condoms many colleges provide on campus. You can snag some at the health center, from your RA, or at your local Planned Parenthood. Set yourself up for success by always keeping some in your backpack, wallet, purse, or in the dresser near your bed.

FYI condoms do expire, so make sure to rotate your stash! Don't use a condom if it seems dry or brittle out of the package or seems iffy at all to you.

Throw a Surprise Party

How many people can you squeeze into a dorm room? Hint: It's a lot more than you might think. College is the perfect time to throw a surprise party because you'll be hard-pressed to find another time in your life where getting a large group of people together is so easy.

Organizing and planning the impromptu get-together is just as fun as the part where you all jump out and yell, "Surprise!" So, break out the streamers and balloons, decorate a cake, and make some party hats. Celebrate your roommate's birthday, or put together a surprise to brighten a fellow student's day just because.

Start a
Podcast

Recording a podcast gives you a fun creative outlet. Plus, if you get enough listeners, you might even start earning some money to pay for all that late-night takeout, or you may discover a passion you want to pursue after graduation. You never know where it could lead!

Your podcast can be about anything you choose. For example, you could create a podcast about dorm life, with insider tips on which buildings are best and why, or strike a more comical tone with stories of ongoing hijinks and campus superstitions unique to your school. You could do it solo, with a few friends, or conduct it interview-style with new guests in every episode.

You can start your podcast with just a smartphone or laptop set up in your dorm room or a quiet common room. Over time, you may decide to improve your "studio" with a microphone or editing software. Once you've gotten comfortable recording your own voice, find a how-to guide online and dive into all the nitty-gritty details of creating and publishing a podcast.

Have a Late-Night Veg-Out with Your Roommate(s)

There are tons of twenty-four-hour places that cater to students, especially near college campuses. So when that 4 a.m. craving for sushi hits, go for it! Invite your roommate(s) to share a pizza while you introduce each other to your all-time favorite movies. Or talk until the early hours of the morning about anything and everything over Chinese takeout. Now's your chance to pig out *and* get to know your roommate(s) better at the same time. These are the types of moments that you'll be able to recall long after you graduate.

Get On Your RA's Good Side

Even though the resident advisor (also called the "resident assistant") for your dorm floor sometimes has to be the enforcer, they're not out to get you. They're simply doing their job. Beyond the title, RAs are normal students like you.

Befriending your RA, or at least developing a relationship built on respect, will only improve the dorm-life experience for you. They can clue you in on what's cool and not cool to do, and even share insider tips, from watching out for a particular RA who's a real stickler to which professors you should take a class with.

Building a good relationship is as simple as being courteous and nice. Make friendly conversation when you see them, keep noise levels down during quiet hours, and avoid blatantly breaking the rules. Don't purposely make your RA's life hard, and you're sure to build good rapport!

Paint Alongside Bob Ross

Bob Ross was the host of a public access show in the eighties that taught people how to paint beautiful landscapes. If you aren't familiar with his show, it might sound a bit corny, but it is oddly relaxing and easy to follow. Ross's calm demeanor and mellow voice, paired with tidbits of positivity and inspiration, have resonated with hundreds—if not thousands—of people through the years, and you can find episodes of his show online with a quick search.

The next time you want to get your mind off of school for a while, break out a canvas and some paint, put on a Bob Ross video, and get to painting happy little trees. Not only will you relieve stress and flex your creative muscles, but you'll also have new art to hang on your dorm wall!

Embrace the Uncomfortable

If the thought of having to share a showering space with dozens of other students makes you feel uncomfortable, you're not alone. But you'll come to realize that while it is a little awkward at first, there isn't anything wrong with the naked body. Best of all, nobody cares. Everyone is changing, showering, and focusing on their own thoughts and feelings, and this general indifference among your peers is ultimately freeing.

Just act like you've been doing this your whole life. Don't stare at anyone and you'll do fine. And as you feel more comfortable with your body around others, you'll start to feel better about yourself, which is a great step forward for your mental health. Being self-conscious is tiring! Letting go of care for what other people think can be a huge relief: It's one less thing to worry about.

The only part of you that should *not* be bare in a communal shower is your feet. Buy some flip-flops to use as dedicated "shower shoes"—any cheap pair will do the trick. The investment is well worth protecting yourself from foot fungus.

Become the Unofficial Leader for Organizing Floor Activities

In a dorm, there are at least fifty to a hundred other people your age looking for something fun to do. Organizing entertaining group activities for your entire floor is easy to do and a great way to feel closer to the people you will see every day for at least the next semester. A tight-knit student community can really elevate your dorm-living experience!

Create a club for discussing books or watching movies once a week. Put together tournaments for everything from trivia and video games to poker and giant Jenga. Have a contest for the best-decorated door with a holiday theme. The possibilities are endless! If you don't have one already, start a *Facebook* group for the entire floor where you can post events, or draw up simple posters and tack them to your floor's bulletin board.

Challenge Yourself to Make Friends with At Least One Person in Every Building

It's common for college campuses to have more than one type of dormitory. The layout of the rooms and how bathrooms are shared (or not shared) varies. It's interesting to get a look at them all, especially if you're thinking about living in the dorms after your freshman year. And beyond differences in physical features, each building has its own unique student community—some are like a tight-knit family while others are more independent. The activities, social happenings, and general atmosphere can vary as well. You might realize that another housing community or dorm setup would be a better fit for you.

As you venture to all areas of the campus, branching out socially will start to become second nature. Making connections is the groundwork of networking, so taking on the challenge to befriend someone in every building will help you practice that skill too.

CHAPTER 2

Making the Most of On-Campus Activities

While your studies do come first, there's so much more to do on campus than just go to class. And while it may seem like you've got plenty of time to see every nook and cranny of the school grounds, your college years fly by—*fast*. Unless you go out of your way to sample as much of it as possible, it's actually pretty easy to miss out on opportunities that you won't find anywhere else. Of course, soaking up all your campus has to offer doesn't mean you have to do *everything*. If you attempt to do that, you'll end up spreading yourself too thin. Instead, you should focus on getting involved with what interests you. And as you learn what activities you really enjoy, you can drop any extras that aren't your thing.

In this chapter, you'll find tons of examples for what you may want to take advantage of while you're on campus. Perks like access to a gym, library, and historic academic buildings, and the feeling of unity that comes from being among fellow students are all things you may miss someday. This chapter is here to help you cover all the bases!

Get to Know All the Buildings Better with a Game of Hide-and-Seek

Make figuring out where everything is (and the fastest ways to get to different buildings) fun by playing a game of hide-and-seek! Form two teams; both will have a chance to be the seekers and the hiders. During each round, time how long it takes the seekers to find all of the hiders. Whichever team of seekers finds the team of hiders fastest is the winner.

Now, the next time you see a frantic student who looks lost, you can swoop in and help them find their class (or resident services or a professor's office) because you know the grounds like the back of your hand.

Practice Field Goal Kicks after Dark

No matter how athletic or unathletic you are, random hijinks like this with your roommate(s) or friend(s) are a great way to blow off some steam and make lasting memories.

Bring more than one football along to your school's football field late at night and take turns standing by the field goal so you don't have to run back and forth every time one of you takes a crack at it. If you don't have access to a football field, you can do a bit of improvising on a more accessible field. Score a goal on the soccer net, or play a round of kickball on the baseball field with a glow-in-the-dark ball.

Be the Model
for an Art Class

College is all about trying new things, some of which may put you outside of your comfort zone. Why is that a good thing? You can learn new things about yourself by stepping outside of that comfortable area, not to mention it's a great confidence booster. Just look at how much you're capable of! And not only is modeling an easy way to step out of your comfort zone while making some money, but it can also help you find a newfound acceptance and love for your body.

Find job postings at your school or talk to the head of the art department. Some classes use a nude model, but if the thought of baring it all totally freaks you out, look for a job that doesn't require complete nudity.

Get Published
in the School Paper

There are lots of ways to get your name, picture, or article published in an issue of your school's paper, and you'll be connecting with the student body in a different way than you normally would. It feels nice to have a little campus-wide notoriety to your name, you can brag about being "published," and it'll look good on your resume. Plus, you'll have a memento of your college days to show kids or grandkids, or take yourself on a solo trip down memory lane whenever you want!

If you like to write, submit a piece of writing. It could be a commentary on the best (and worst) foods in the cafeteria, a column where you dole out advice to students each week, or whatever else you can dream up. If writing isn't your thing, you can organize an event that garners attention, or ask the editor if they're looking for unique content on a particular topic. You can usually find submission guidelines on your school's website or the website for the periodical itself.

Go to at Least
Five Club Callouts

Look at all the weird, intriguing, and super-niche clubs offered at your college. You're virtually guaranteed to find one that speaks to your own interests (or helps you discover a new interest!).

Some clubs you might find on your campus include:

- Hiking Club

- Medieval Reenactment Club

- Off-Roading Club

- Bad Movie Trivia Club

- Latin/Ballroom/Swing Dance Club

- Paintball Club

- *Dungeons & Dragons* Club

- Knitting/Crocheting Club

- Baking Club

- Yelling Club

Go to callouts for at least five of these clubs to get a better idea of what each one is like, and commit to joining one (or more, if you decide) of them. Beyond enjoying a hobby, participating in a club is a great way to meet new people with similar interests. Additionally, professional clubs can provide unique opportunities. For example, many professional organizations have scholarships that only accept applications from student members.

Try Every Item on the Dining Hall Menu

The dining hall at your school likely offers a huge selection of food. It can honestly be overwhelming at first! It's understandable to find yourself paralyzed by the overload of choices presented on the menu, often opting for the most familiar ones.

Once you get past the initial shock though, the dining hall is another great way to expand your horizons (or, in this case, your taste buds). You can try a whole host of food you normally wouldn't order, as well as come up with your own innovative hacks (how about waffle-iron mac 'n' cheese?) with the ingredients that are available. Of course, trying everything offered on the menu at least once is quite the challenge, but you can chip away at it each day and have fun while you're at it.

Take a picture of the menu or save a screenshot from your school's website. Then every time you eat something new, draw a checkmark on the photo in your phone gallery or an editing app to keep track of your progress. Revolutionize your everyday meals in the best of ways!

Watch the Sunset from the Tallest Building on Campus

Even if you have a nice view from your dorm room window, you may get a little tired of it from time to time. (Especially if it ends up being the frequent backdrop for less exciting things like studying.) Revitalize your weary eyes with a new look at the grounds. A whole new perspective can shake up your everyday routine. With a bird's-eye view, you may spot an unexplored part of campus, or discover a shortcut to one of your classes.

Finding the tallest building will be pretty easy, but getting to the top of it could be a little adventure in itself. Will you be able to get access to the roof? Or will you need to hunt down the best facing window on the top floor?

Either way, the reward of your efforts will be enjoying a great view with a beautiful sunset. As an added bonus, now you'll have a cool spot to share when you want to set the mood for romance.

Attend a Lecture You're Not Enrolled In

Pick a class on a topic you have an interest in but know little or nothing about, and either sit in on a lecture or audit the class.

Only in a class where you don't need to diligently scribble down notes and worry about passing tests can you have a true, unadulterated learning experience. Appreciate the lecture purely for the sake of expanding your knowledge. At the end, you may decide to sign up for the class (or other classes on that topic) or even consider a change in major.

Participate in a Wacky Tradition

Playing in the annual prom dress rugby game? Jumping in a freezing cold lake at midnight? There will be tons of opportunities for you to get in on a school-wide tradition or two during the academic year. Many of them happen during freshman week, at homecoming, and before/after football games. Sororities and fraternities are a hotspot for established practices as well. Ask upperclassmen for the inside scoop on the best ones or look online for more details.

As crazy as some of these traditions can seem, they build a sense of camaraderie with the whole student body that's hard to replicate elsewhere. Being united in a funny or downright bizarre activity is a feeling every student should experience at least once. Plus, you'll have something you and your friends can laugh about later!

Watch a Production by a Lesser-Known Club or Organization

Watching a show can be a source of entertainment for a night, but it can also stimulate and revitalize your own creativity. Have you seen a live play or orchestra perform before? It's different than watching one on TV. The experience is more immersive, and often your emotional response is elevated too. No two performances are exactly the same. You may discover a new love for musicals, ballets, plays, or other performance art that you otherwise wouldn't have if you never watched a production in person!

As a bonus, you'll be supporting your fellow students in their passion. They work hard to put on a good show and love having an audience. Bring a bouquet of flowers and toss them on stage at curtain call or congratulate each performer after the show.

Strike a Pose with Your School Mascot

Nothing says school pride more than taking an enthusiastic picture with your mascot! Whether you're feeling stressed over a bad grade, fighting off homesickness, or just looking for a little memento of your college years, a quick photo shoot with your school's mascot is sure to make you appreciate the great opportunities around every corner.

You can find the mascot at any major sporting event or even walking around campus. Whip out your phone for a selfie or hand the camera to a friend, and have fun with your pose: Give them a big hug, a fist bump, or, if you're feeling a little daring, a kiss on the cheek. You could even ask them to pick you up bridal style (or vice versa), jump in the air together, or pose like Charlie's Angels. Be silly and have fun with it!

Organize an Awesome Theme Party

Forget run-of-the-mill, balloons-and-streamers parties: Themed parties are where the real fun's at. And unique nights like these are the ones you'll remember most after college.

Some ideas include:

- Foam party: There's music, dancing, and, of course, foam. You'll need a foam machine (which can be rented from a party store) for this one, but it's totally worth it!
- Highlighter party (also known as a black-light party): Guests wear white T-shirts and color on each other with highlighters, which makes everyone glow under the black light.
- Meme party: Everyone dresses up as their favorite meme.

Creativity is key in planning a great theme party, so let your imagination run wild!

Eye-Bomb Five Things Around Campus

Eye-bombing is the act of personifying everyday objects by putting googly eyes on them. It's a fun way to appreciate things on campus that you may otherwise pass without a second thought, and to spread unexpected humor to anyone who notices your handiwork. The more preposterous the location the better!

Buy an assortment of googly eyes (the kind with sticky backing) ranging from small to extra large. Then spend a free afternoon going around campus with a friend or two looking for things that would be enhanced by a pair of wobbly eyes.

For example, you could stick them on:

- A statue
- A poster with people
- A tree with a knot that looks like a mouth or nose
- A public water fountain (just above where the water shoots out)
- A picture of a burger in the dining hall
- Your roommate's can of soda in the mini-fridge

Eye-bombing can be an amusing ongoing hobby you do on your own as well. Keep a small bag of googly eyes in your backpack so you can "strike" whenever you come across the perfect inanimate object.

Give an
Admissions Tour

Put your school knowledge (and multitasking skills) to the test and share what everyday life as a college student is like with prospective students touring the campus. What's there to do on the weekends? What unique and maybe even unusual classes have you taken? Tell groups what dorm living is actually like, what you like best (and least) about your school, and other information you'd tell your freshman self if you could go back in time. Your honest experience as a student is immensely valuable to those about to begin their undergraduate career. You may even learn a few new things about the school yourself when you start prepping for tours!

As an added bonus, colleges usually pay tour guides (though sometimes it's strictly on a volunteer basis). Ask for an application at the admission's office to apply for the job. Tip: Dressing and acting professionally can help you land the position.

Score a Free T-Shirt at a School Game

Many colleges have T-shirt cannons they use to shoot T-shirts into the crowd at different sports games. You can catch the attention of the student operating it by standing up and making a lot of noise. Of course, these cannons are far from accurate, so scoring a shirt may be more about luck than anything else. But if you do get lucky, you've not only landed yourself a free shirt (who doesn't love free stuff?), but you'll also have a pretty cool bit of trivia to share about yourself at parties.

Host or Participate in a Watermelon-Eating Contest

Participants, a table for them to sit at, and lots of watermelon are all you'll need for this hilarious, chaotic competition. A plastic tablecloth will also make cleanup afterward easier, but it isn't absolutely necessary. (Keep in mind that this contest is best done when watermelons are in season, as in-season fruit is cheaper than out-of-season fruit.)

If you're the one organizing the event, you'll want to slice the watermelons into thirds or fourths to create large wedges. The winner will be the person who eats their slice of watermelon down to the rind the fastest. The twist is that no hands are allowed, so have contestants put their hands behind their back while eating.

You can do this with a small group of friends, or, if you're feeling ambitious, you can organize a larger contest with your entire dorm floor, resident hall, or anyone on campus who's down for a tasty challenge. Pit the winners of multiple rounds against each other to determine who is the ultimate armless watermelon-eating champ and bestow them with a crown carved from a watermelon rind. Or whatever silly prize you can conjure up!

Investigate Your Campus at Night for Hidden Gems

Is there really a tunnel system that runs underneath the whole campus? What's in that unused floor of the old academic building? Can you find the hidden room in the basement of the library?

Whether you have a small campus or a sprawling one, there's sure to be a few things you haven't seen before. Satisfy your curiosity by doing some poking around. Exploring at night will give you more freedom and make things more interesting. Just be sure to bring at least one pal and a flashlight!

Play a Game of Eighties-Inspired Volleyball with Your Squad

There's a time and a place for everything, including the weird and slightly crazy. And when you're faced with two choices as an undergrad, always pick the one that will give you the best story. After all, you're not just here for the degree: You're also here for the experiences you'll remember for years to come. So, in this scenario, if you have the option to play a normal round of volleyball or an eighties-style match, you know what to choose.

Sport neon tights with leg warmers—and don't forget the headband. Bring the energy, overexaggerate when you spike the ball, and, of course, blast your favorite eighties tunes. Who cares what anyone thinks (although chances are this isn't the craziest thing they've seen this week—it's college!)? You and your friends are just out in the quad having a good time.

Act Like a Kid Again

Elementary students and college students have at least one thing in common: a secret hope that they'll get a snow day (or five) during the winter. If your campus is located somewhere where it snows, remember what it's like to be a kid again and make the most of it the next time there's fresh powder on the ground. Start a snowball fight, make a snow angel, and build a snowman! Or borrow a tray from the dining hall to go "traybogganing" down a hill. A garbage bag over a piece of cardboard works surprisingly well as a make-shift sled too.

If it doesn't snow in your area, there are other easy ways to tap into your inner child, like raking up and then jumping into a huge pile of leaves or pulling on your rain boots and going puddle-jumping. Take joy in simply being unconcerned with adult stresses for a while.

Sit Back and People-Watch

Park yourself on a bench outside or set up camp in the dining hall with some snacks and spend a morning, afternoon, or evening observing students and staff as they go about their lives. Watching people when they think no one is looking or listening can be quite fascinating. There are lots of little nuances you can pick up on that you'd normally miss because you weren't taking the time to notice. It's an entertaining and relaxing way to spend some free time, but it can also help you be a more empathetic person because it's a reminder that every person is living a life just as complex as your own.

Meet Classmates from Different Countries

The world is a big place full of interesting people with cultures similar to, as well as very different from, the one you're used to. The opportunity to interact with foreign students is super-rewarding: You both have something you can learn from each other. Get the most out of college by expanding your knowledge beyond books and tests and reach out to students from other countries. Give them the warm welcome you would want if you were in a foreign country. Who knows, you might make some good friends! See how many different countries you can meet students from in your classes, social events, and extracurriculars.

Make a Funnellator or Trebuchet to Catapult Water Balloons

There's something satisfying about flinging things as far as you can and watching them go *splat*. And part of the fun is crafting the throwing device of your choice. A funnellator is essentially a large funnel attached to a rubber hose or surgical tubing. Building a trebuchet (a catapult with a long throwing arm) will take a little longer, but the payoff is arguably even better. It's simple enough to do by following an online video with a few additional supplies. If you want some assistance, just seek out an engineering major to help you with your medieval siege engine.

Once your contraption is ready, it's time to start a water balloon fight! Get friends—or anyone who wants in on the fun—together and find an open area where you can have at it without worrying about hitting someone who isn't part of the fight.

If you're more interested in catapulting your balloons as far away as you can, rather than battling over the football field, water balloons aren't the only thing you can send flying off into the distance. Eggs are pretty satisfying too. Try different projectiles, compare your results, take notes, perfect your craft, and maybe even start a new club.

DJ a Silent Disco in the Library

The only way you can have a party in the library is if it's quiet. The solution: a silent disco, where everyone wears headphones and dances to the same playlist. It's a unique, often unifying experience to try at least once. Clubs use special headphones, but you can pull it off with a DIY setup that allows everyone to use their own personal earbuds. Put together a sweet mix of songs and then spread the word by passing out flyers, telling your friends, or making a posting on the school bulletin board.

Host a
Friendsgiving

Instead of going your separate ways for Thanksgiving, spend it together one year and host a "Friendsgiving." Make it a potluck-style event where everyone can bring their favorite traditional dish. Or have fun cobbling together your own special meal with just the microwave in your dorm and a hot plate. Also consider inviting students who don't have a home to go back to for the holidays.

For activities, you can create a group gratitude list, decorate sugar cookies, play a board game, put on *A Charlie Brown Thanksgiving*, or play a game of flag football in the quad. Enjoy each other's company before slipping into a post-feast food coma. Your college years go by quickly, so soak up as much friend time as you can and be sure to take a group photo. Friendsgiving will be a great day to reminisce over for years to come!

Express Yourself with Sidewalk Chalk Art

Sidewalk chalk is good ol' wholesome fun. It also has that nostalgia factor, as it brings you back to when you were a kid and things were simpler. Design a cool mural, create a game of hopscotch, or leave inspiring messages to spread positivity to students as they bustle around campus. Chalking is also a great way to announce events you want to get the word out about.

Check your school's website for their policies on sidewalk chalk; it should outline designated areas where you're free to do it. One word of advice: Buy chalk anywhere *but* the university bookstore; it's usually overpriced.

Uncover Cool Treasure While Geocaching

Geocaches are hidden containers that you can find all around the world, including on your college campus. It's a fascinating hobby enjoyed by many and definitely worth giving a shot. Locations are marked by GPS coordinates, so the challenge is to use your navigational skills to find them. Each geocache has a little bit of "treasure" left inside of it—you never know what you'll find! Basically, geocaching is as close as you can get to being a modern-day pirate without sailing the seven seas. The golden rule of geocaching is that if you take what's inside, you leave something of equal (or greater) value as a replacement.

You can get started by using a free app on your phone or a GPS receiver like a Garmin watch. It's recommended that you read some tips online or watch a video so you have an idea of what to look for before starting your first geocaching adventure. You may be surprised at just how many nearby geocaches there are, so get out there and find some booty!

Look at Your School from a New Perspective with a Campus Job

You should absolutely get a job at some point while you're attending college; the worst thing you can do is graduate without any experience besides your degree. Just like book smarts and street smarts, there's a difference between theoretical knowledge and practical application. Both are important, but employers tend to value applicants with in-field experience over those armed only with a classroom understanding. Being able to include real-world know-how on your resume will help it stand out among the flood of new graduates holding the same degree. It's also pretty nice to not be completely broke all the time.

Sure, there are a lot of jobs offered off campus, but here are some reasons to get a job *on* campus:

- **Proximity:** You won't lose any time to commuting

- **Socializing:** It's a good way to meet other students and possibly make new friends

- **Flexibility:** The school will be more understanding about your schedule and willing to work around it

Additionally, seeing everything about your school (including staff and students) from a totally different perspective can be pretty interesting!

Dining halls, maintenance, and administrative offices are commonly hiring, and they usually offer ten to twenty hours per week. Pick a job that you can comfortably handle—one that won't interfere with your studies. Maybe you won't have a job for the entire time you're at college; however, any working experience will look good on a resume and, more importantly, will help you make better decisions about your future in the working world.

Create Your Own Bucket List

- ☐ _____
- ☐ _____
- ☐ _____
- ☐ _____
- ☐ _____
- ☐ _____
- ☐ _____
- ☐ _____
- ☐ _____
- ☐ _____
- ☐ _____
- ☐ _____
- ☐ _____
- ☐ _____
- ☐ _____
- ☐ _____
- ☐ _____
- ☐ _____

- [ ] _____
- [ ] _____
- [ ] _____
- [ ] _____
- [ ] _____
- [ ] _____
- [ ] _____
- [ ] _____
- [ ] _____
- [ ] _____
- [ ] _____
- [ ] _____
- [ ] _____
- [ ] _____
- [ ] _____
- [ ] _____
- [ ] _____
- [ ] _____
- [ ] _____
- [ ] _____

CHAPTER 3

Adventuring in Town (and Beyond)

College is kind of a paradox: It's when you simultaneously have the most and least responsibility. The most because you have more independence and control over your choices than ever before. And the least because this is only the beginning. After graduation, you'll have to split your time between work, personal commitments, and adult stuff—which means less time left over for other activities. College can be one of the most carefree times in your life. It's your chance to do the things you've always wanted to do while you're not bogged down with a million other responsibilities. Of course, you may be thinking, "Easier said than done when you're broke!" Thankfully, there are tons of things you can do without breaking the bank.

This chapter is chock-full of ideas for making the most out of your free time (and limited funds). You'll discover the value of an open mind when it comes to things you wouldn't normally consider, how important relaxation is for your well-being, and that sometimes it's the little things that nourish your soul the most. Variety is the spice of life, so it's time to do something (actually, many somethings) you'll remember long after graduation!

Road-Trip to an Away Game

Going to a college sports game is an incredible experience (even if you're not all that into sports or barely understand the rules). From cheering on talented students to the greasy concession stand food and air thick with a contagious energy, college sporting events are a delight for all your senses. Outside of your friend group, the crowd may be full of strangers, yet you can't help but feel unified in the "us versus them" mentality. You can participate in age-old traditions, sing chants, and yell like a crazy fan all in the name of school spirit. Combine that with an impromptu road trip with friends and you've got yourself an amazing time!

Do you know anyone at (or near) the rival school? Maybe a friend from high school is a student there. Or a family friend lives in the area. Send them a message to see if they have a couch you can crash on after the game. And if that doesn't pan out, you can always set up camp in your car for a night: It will be an even more adventurous trip you're sure to remember for years to come.

Go to a
Renaissance Fair

Whether you go in costume or jeans and a T-shirt, watching amateur jousting while snacking on a giant turkey leg is an experience worth having at least once during college. You might find you've discovered a whole new interest to enjoy during free weekends, see your English lit course come to life, or just have a great day getting away from homework and bonding with roommates. Enjoy it for the wildly unique event that it is—just don't forget the sunscreen!

Enjoy a Warm Doughnut in the Early Hours after a Party

Holding a doughnut fresh from the oven while laughing with your friends about the events of the past few hours might just be the perfect way to end a night. Go right when the local shop opens so you know the doughnuts are as fresh as fresh gets. The satisfaction you'll get from biting into the deep-fried ring of your choice after a full night of hijinks is completely different than if you had just woken up super-early to get breakfast. It's an experience that will give you a whole new appreciation for the humble doughnut—and the little moments during college that no one really talks about.

Travel by Train to Somewhere New

During your college years, the desire to travel is strong, but funds are usually low. However, there are alternatives to an expensive plane ticket—like traveling by train. Riding the rails isn't the fastest way to get from point A to point B, but compared to air travel it's more comfortable (hello, legroom), generally more affordable, and way less stressful.

Take a short train ride to the next city over (or a nearby place you haven't visited before) and savor the experience just as much as the destination. The windows on trains are big, and train tracks go where the highways don't, which means there will be plenty of scenic views. Train travel is best enjoyed when you're not in a rush, so plan accordingly to keep the mood of the trip laid-back.

Watch a Movie at a Drive-In Theater

Yes, drive-in theaters still exist! And a surprising amount of them are operating; hop online to find the one that's nearest to you. Double features are common at drive-ins, so it's like getting twice the value compared to a normal theater. Maximize your money by going on a night when they charge by the car instead of by the person.

The movie itself isn't the main attraction, though. Outdoor theaters are about the full experience. A trip to a drive-in is like traveling back to a different period in time. And before the movie starts playing it's more of a social event, similar to tailgating only without the grills.

Load up on snacks, bring a group of friends, and get there at least thirty minutes early to chat, maybe toss around a Frisbee, or even kick around a soccer ball before the movie. If you or any of your friends have a pickup truck, consider getting an air mattress or two to put in the truck bed, then cover it with blankets and pillows for a cozy place to sit back and enjoy the evening.

Tip: Turn on your car in between features to keep your battery from going dead by the end of the night.

Spend a Day Floating Down a River

River tubing is a lazy but highly rewarding way to spend a hot day. You get to slather on the sunscreen, soak up the sun, splash around in the water, and enjoy the scenery. If you want to do something more active, rafting and kayaking are a blast, and you'll still have plenty of opportunities to chill.

You can buy your own tube and life jacket or rent them from an outfitter. Schools typically offer discount programs for activities like this, so be sure to look into it when planning your trip. Outfitters also have shuttles that drop you off and pick you up at the end of the day.

A little preparation will help make sure your river floating is nothing short of delightful. Look into rivers near you that are best for floating, the expected conditions day of (so you don't waste a trip out just to turn back because of a storm), and what essentials to bring with you.

Tubing is a classic pastime for a reason. It leaves you feeling exhausted by the end of the day, but in a satisfying "I'm gonna sleep really good tonight" kind of way.

Do Something Spontaneous

College is the perfect time to be a little wild. You've got the time and access to tons of new experiences, so why not do the things you've always wanted to do? Jump at the chance to try something purely for the sake of novelty.

Instead of picking a date ahead of time, make it a spur-of-the-moment decision. It will feel like even more of an adventure! So-and-so mentions they want to go cliff diving and you're not busy? Look up the nearest location to see where you can do it safely that day. Your best friend's parents gifted ziplining tickets to share? Without a doubt you're in! Your roommates dare you to skinny-dip with them? Here goes nothing!

There could be an adrenaline junkie inside of you, so give it a whirl. It may even turn out to be a favorite pastime. You'll never know unless you make the leap at least once.

Attend a Murder Mystery Dinner Party

With the right people, a game of solving a murder mystery is a total blast. You get to dress up in costumes, engage in role-play, and, most importantly, catch the killer. The more everyone gets into it, the more fun you'll all have. Putting together your own dinner party is easy to do with the help of an online guide or inexpensive kit. Or you can buy a ticket to a local dinner theater show where actors are a part of the game. (Check your school's website for possible discounts.) By the end of the night, you may have a new obsession with role-playing games, true crime, doing detective work, or all of these things.

Stargaze at an Observatory or Planetarium

You don't need to be an astronomy major to appreciate a spectacular night sky! Take an after-dark trip to look at something cool through a giant telescope or see a projection of a celestial scene. Your university might have an observatory or planetarium—if not, there's likely one nearby.

Visiting an observatory or planetarium is sure to spark your sense of wonder and curiosity. There is *so* much to know about space, and the astronomy enthusiasts there are more than happy to tell you anything you want to know. It's a fun way to learn more about the stars. Use your newfound knowledge to impress your crush with a fact or two on a stargazing date!

Go On an Adventure in Nature

When school has you feeling frazzled and overworked, there's nothing like a little fresh air to clear your mind and revitalize your energy. And the beauty of it is that there are endless ways to enjoy the great outdoors! You could visit an arboretum, hike to a waterfall, explore a botanical garden, check out a natural landmark, or even soak in a natural hot spring.

The subtle art of recharging your batteries is an underrated but much needed life skill. Practice it often now to have it mastered before setting out into the working world, and you'll avoid future burnout.

Hit the Open Road for an Unplanned Trip

Road trips might be a college cliché, but for good reason: They're fun and full of moments you'll remember for years to come. Plus, when else are you going to have this much free time? You'll most certainly take a few road trips as an undergrad; for one of them, pick a direction to head and see where you end up. Without a point B to get to, you won't have any feelings of being rushed. This will open you up to stopping at whatever cool things catch your eye. Be sure to take all those interesting detours! Check out the weird roadside attractions to get your picture taken and browse the unique shops in the middle of nowhere.

An unplanned road trip is about learning how to find joy in the journey. So relish getting lost in conversation for hours, singing along with your friends, eating gas station snacks, and thinking about everything and anything. Understanding how much of your life is affected by your attitude is a lesson you can take with you long after graduation.

Share a Slice of Pie at a Diner in the Middle of the Night

Late nights and college go together like grilled cheese sandwiches and tomato soup. Between study sessions and the freedom to go to bed whenever you want, there are plenty of reasons to be up past midnight. Take one of these opportunities to head to a twenty-four-hour diner in the middle of the night with your friends. Enjoy a slice of pie, or perhaps some greasy food or mugs of coffee, and laugh as loudly as you please in the deserted atmosphere. Little moments like these, where you can enjoy being lighthearted, hold a certain kind of magic that leaves a lasting impression.

See What Roller Derby Is All About

Roller derby: It's like going to the roller rink when you were a kid, only with a lot more excitement and skaters colliding with each other on purpose. With two teams of athletic and highly competitive women, it's hard to take your eyes off this full-contact sport once a match starts. Go to a game, cheer for your favorite "jammer," and enjoy being taken in by the chaotic, energetic spirit of both the players and the crowd.

Watching a roller derby match is an activity where you can have a blast with friends or roommates and be exposed to something new at the same time. So, when you feel like the hangout routine is getting a little too predictable, shake things up!

Zen Out in a Sensory Deprivation Tank

A sensory deprivation tank (also known as a float tank or isolation pod) may sound like something you'd find in a sci-fi movie, but it's actually comparable to a soundproof bathtub. The water inside is filled with thousands of pounds of Epsom salts to make floating on your back completely effortless. When you close your eyes, it becomes harder and harder to differentiate your limbs from the skin-temperature water until you're left with a zero-gravity feeling.

When was the last time *you* went without your sense of touch, sound, or sight? (Much less all three at once!) Removing external stimuli gives your brain a break it wouldn't normally have, which is great for easing stress, boosting your mood, and avoiding burnout amid essays and exams. In fact, a sixty-minute float session is proven to help you reduce anxiety, relieve stress, and achieve deep relaxation. Some people also claim sensory deprivation is how you can take meditation to the "next level."

Look up float spas near you to try out this unique activity; you might discover it's your new favorite way to unwind.

Go Mini Golfing in Full Golfing Gear

Whether you haven't played mini golf since you were a kid, or played last week, it's time to put a new spin on a nostalgic favorite. Professional golfer style is easy to copy: You just need a polo top, chinos, and a flat cap. Put on your game face to really sell the whole look, and learn a few golf slang terms beforehand to toss around for good measure.

Not only is this a fun and cheap activity to do with your friends on a free weeknight or weekend day, but it also makes for a creative group date. You can pair up, talk trash, and get competitive over who can finish the putt-putt course in the least amount of strokes. And regardless of who wins the game, you can all look forward to cooling off with an ice cream cone afterward.

Spend a Day Biking Around Town

There are tons of exotic locations that might come to mind when you're putting together a bucket list, but your college town can have a lot to offer too! Plus, it's readily available for you to explore without breaking the bank.

There are sure to be parts of the surrounding area you're unfamiliar with. Unless you go out of your way to traverse it, you may never discover what makes your college town interesting and different from all the rest. Rent a bike for the day (if you don't own one) and get familiar with all of the parts of the area that make it special. A little exercise always pairs well with sightseeing.

Explore a Forgotten Location

Even as the world gets busier and more populated, deserted places continue to exist and intrigue. Empty malls, abandoned mental institutions, old amusement parks, and long-forgotten mining towns all hold fascinating stories.

Maybe you spotted a deserted building on your way to grab a coffee in town. Or you've heard about a nearby location that's rumored to be haunted and you're itching to investigate it. It's time for a little detective work! Just be sure to do a little research *before* you start poking around. Find out if the location is open to the public, and consider bringing a friend along. It's always best to explore during the day as well. Urban exploration (a.k.a. "Urbex" or UE) can be a neat hobby as long as you're safe and smart about it.

Take a Well-Planned Weekend Getaway

Your college years are when you have the ability to feed your spontaneous side with reckless abandon. Though, after the umpteenth time of wishing you had thought to grab your toothbrush before heading out—or that you had at least set a max spending amount before your bank balance started looking a little *too* sparse—you may tire of every trip being last minute. Learning how to plan and budget are valuable skills, and a weekend getaway is excellent practice!

Choose a location you'd really love to visit that is within your price range (or will be after a little saving). Figure out what you want to do and see there, how far the drive is, where you'll stay overnight, and who you'll go with. Decide on if you'll be eating out for every meal or taking along a cooler packed with food. Calculate the total costs and set aside or save up the funds accordingly. Whether you over-prepare, under-prepare, or get it right on your first shot, it's all part of the learning experience! Spur-of-the-moment and planned outings have different perks; discover which type you love most by experimenting with both.

Try Ice Blocking

Ice blocking—essentially snowless sledding—is a fun, often hilarious activity that's perfect for warmer climates and weather. You just need a large block of ice, a towel, and a somewhat steep, grassy hill. You can get blocks of ice from a supermarket, or if you have a large enough freezer, you can use a plastic storage container as a mold (four inches of water should be plenty thick). Plan to get dirty and wear clothes you don't care about!

Now for the fun: Put the ice block at the top of the hill, lay your towel on top, sit on the towel (while holding onto the corners), and start sliding. It can be a bit of a challenge at first as the ice tends to spin; there's an art to mastering control of it with your towel. You can ride down the hill solo, create a human "train," attempt to ride the ice like a surfboard, or try whatever crazy tricks come to mind.

Go Out for an Epic Brunch

Step aside, breakfast, because *brunch* is the most important meal of the day. Going out for brunch is the perfect lazy weekend activity. You don't have to rush to get up in the morning, nor do you have to wait until later to eat. You get to sleep in, enjoy a smorgasbord of delicious food, and catch up with friends.

Plus after a night of fun, there's nothing like breakfast and lunch rolled into one perfect buffet to put the pep back in your step! Put on your "Sunday best," go to the trendiest brunch spot in town (the one with the long line out front), and see what all the hype is about. Act like you're a food blogger: Choose something based on its visual presentation, snap some drool-worthy pics, and share them on social media captioned with your best impression of a restaurant critique.

Lay Out under a Meteor Shower

Meteor showers are one of those events you just have to experience at least once. Stars are literally falling across the sky! It's a beautiful sight that fortunately happens on a few occasions throughout each year—so there's no excuse to miss one.

Head out to an open field near campus on the night of a meteor shower and set up camp with a big blanket and snacks on the grass. (If it's a little chilly, find a place to park where you have a great view of the sky, and watch from the comfort of your heated car.) Bring a friend or date and bond over good conversation as you enjoy the mystic beauty of cosmic debris together.

Take In the Sights at an Oddly Specific Local Festival

Unless you're looking for them, you may never realize just how many different festivals are held every year. Even if your college town is rather small, you may find yourself surprised by the variety of celebrations happening right under your nose. From cherry blossom and floating lantern festivals to waterfront float parades, UFO spaceship landing parties, and soapbox derbies, you're sure to discover a fun (and possibly bizarre) local event that tickles your fancy.

Delight in the opportunity to experience something truly divergent from the status quo! There's also a strong possibility you'll learn something new, like the origin of the celebration or the weird history of the town itself.

Check Out an Open Mic Night

College is a great time to expose yourself to tons of experiences that are normally off your beaten path. At an open mic night, you get to soak in live music with a unique local flavor. It's a hangout for budding artists with all ranges of skills who are from all walks of life. Anyone can get on stage (including you), and every open mic night is different—that's what keeps it so interesting.

Look online to find open mic events in your area. Pick one that catches your eye and enjoy the night with an open mind! You may discover a cool new genre of music, fall in love with the atmosphere itself, or be inspired to start writing your own songs. Remember it takes a lot of guts to perform on stage; the musicians always appreciate a little positivity and encouragement!

Dine Out Based on the Recommendation of a Stranger

Go downtown or to another restaurant-heavy part of town. Ask someone walking by where they like to eat and what they like to order, then go there. If they recommend somewhere you've eaten before, thank them and get a suggestion from another passerby.

This is a great way for you and your friends to further explore your college town. It's like a game of chance because you never know where you'll end up. If the stranger is a local, they may direct you to an amazing eatery that few visitors know about. If the person is a visitor themselves, you may be pointed toward a restaurant they just ate at and enjoyed. Either way, you'll get to branch out from your usual favorites and maybe check out a different area of town, interact with someone new, and, of course, eat food!

Spend a Day Pretending You Go to a Different School

Pile some of your new college buddies in the car to take along with you for a trip to a high school friend's campus! It goes both ways: When they visit their high school friends, you get to tag along. You'll get to check out the differences between college campuses, and maybe the surrounding area, too, as your new friends get acquainted with your hometown pals—under the super-secret guise of being students there yourselves.

If you feel like you're starting to drift apart from the friends you grew up with, this activity can help you reconnect and rekindle your flames of friendship. And even if you and your BFF are rock solid, it's always great to see each other in person! Time and effort are important parts of long-lasting friendships; make sure the people in your life know how much you value them!

Fly a Kite
on a Windy Day

From getting your kite up in the air to learning how to maneuver it for cool tricks, kite flying is a pastime that will keep you on your toes. Part of the fun is simply watching the kite do its thing in the air!

Kite flying is an inexpensive hobby to try out. After the kite, all you need is a windy location to practice your skills. The beach is a popular destination for kite flyers; don't be afraid to strike up a conversation with others nearby. Usually, these hobbyists love nothing more than to share their passion for flying kites and they're happy to answer any questions you may have.

Believe it or not, there are also multiple types of kites. From delta kites to Rokkakus to cellular kites and more, there's sure to be at least one that's calling your name. You may be able to score one for super-cheap at a garage sale, on *Craigslist*, or on a local online resale group. Give it a try—you might discover that kite flying is your new favorite hobby, find it oddly cathartic, or just get a kick out of sharing tricks with your friends.

Have a Local Eatery Taste Test

One of the simple joys in life is grabbing something to eat at a local restaurant, café, or food truck. Each town has something unique to offer that you won't find anywhere else. And there's nothing like chatting with friends while sharing a delicious bite!

Get to know your campus surroundings better by going on a tour of local eateries with your friends and rating each one. Everyone might have their own opinions of which places stand out, or you may end up with a crowd favorite to revisit again and again.

Create Your Own Bucket List

- [ ] _____
- [ ] _____
- [ ] _____
- [ ] _____
- [ ] _____
- [ ] _____
- [ ] _____
- [ ] _____
- [ ] _____
- [ ] _____
- [ ] _____
- [ ] _____
- [ ] _____
- [ ] _____
- [ ] _____
- [ ] _____
- [ ] _____
- [ ] _____

- [ ] _____
- [ ] _____
- [ ] _____
- [ ] _____
- [ ] _____
- [ ] _____
- [ ] _____
- [ ] _____
- [ ] _____
- [ ] _____
- [ ] _____
- [ ] _____
- [ ] _____
- [ ] _____
- [ ] _____
- [ ] _____
- [ ] _____
- [ ] _____
- [ ] _____
- [ ] _____

Rounding Out Academics

When it comes to schooling, the best way to approach it is to treat it like a job. Not only will this mindset make your eventual transition to a full-time job easier, but it also helps you in achieving a healthy balance. Stress-free leisure time, because you got all your assignments done well before the last minute, is an added bonus. Academic goals aren't as glaringly obvious as other ambitions you may have as a college student. Even so, you can come up with subtle ways to take some of the pain out of studying, set yourself up for adult success, and elevate your all-around learning experience. It doesn't take much to go above and beyond, but it can make a big difference.

This chapter is packed full of little ways to get that extra *oomph* out of your academic life. You'll find ideas for maximizing productivity, getting on your professor's good side, building confidence, planning for the future, and, at the end of the day, not taking yourself too seriously. Try out different activities to figure out which ones are the best fit for you.

Discover Where Your Classes Are with a Game of Building Tag

No one likes getting to a class late on the first day and facing a sea of students all staring—much less a disapproving professor. Figure out where your classes are ahead of time, and have some fun along the way, with a game of building tag with your friends. To play, each of you will race to find your class locations, taking a selfie of yourselves beside each room number as proof for the other players. Be sure to bring along a list of your classes so you can check off each one as you find it. You can also bring a campus map marked with each class location to help you find them faster. Whoever wins gets a reward of your choosing!

Dress Up (Instead of Down) for a Final Exam

As a college student, you can't be told how to dress (well, at least within the school dress code). So, like many other students, a robe or onesie pajamas and bunny slippers may be your go-to choice on exam days. It's hard to resist the temptation of sleeping in for an extra twenty minutes—instead of pulling on pants and combing your hair—when you know you can get away with it.

Of course, there's nothing wrong with being comfortable. But you might be surprised to learn that putting some effort into your appearance can actually help you perform better on an exam. You don't have to strut in wearing a tuxedo (unless you want to), but dressing a little nicer than you normally would can give you a confidence boost and may even help reduce some of the pre-test jitters.

Combine All of Your Syllabi Into One Calendar So You Never Miss a Beat

Go through the syllabus of each of your classes and write down every single assignment, little and big, in an academic-year planner, an oversized desk pad calendar, or digital calendar app on your phone. Combining all of your due dates for every class into one master calendar makes it easy to stay on top of everything. You can then use your calendar to plan out assignments ahead of time, so instead of remembering on Sunday night that there is a paper due on Monday morning and racing through the night to get it done, you'll have it ready to go—maybe even a week or more in advance.

Take a Course in a Less Expected Language

Learning a second language is an extremely marketable skill. Being bilingual will almost certainly give you a leg up career-wise. But knowing a less traditional language can make you even *more* competitive in the job market. Not to mention it is a fun way to get in some of electives needed to graduate.

Consider signing up for a class (either on campus or online) in:

- A nonverbal language like ASL or Morse code
- A fantasy language like Klingon or Elvish
- A language with a critical need in professional fields such as Arabic, Punjabi, or Chinese
- A Celtic language like Gaelic or Welsh
- A "dead" language like ancient Greek or Latin
- An indigenous language like Cherokee, Navajo, Maori, or Hawaiian

It's unlikely you'll be able to devote this much time and effort to learning a language again, much less have the motivation. Seize the opportunity while you have the chance!

Sit In On As Many Free Guest Talks As You Can

There will be more than a few seminars given by guest speakers on campus. These talks are open to any student who wants to attend, no matter what classes you're enrolled in. The guest speakers may be alumni, experts, or esteemed people in their field.

Listening in on guest talks is a great—and free—way to learn about some pretty cool topics. Maybe you'll discover what projects researchers in your field are working on, or hear the inspiring story of a life-changing experience. You might even realize a new passion or career you want to pursue after graduation, just by listening in on a single guest talk!

Make a Friend in Each of Your Classes

Even if you're not purposely skipping, there will likely come a day when you aren't able to make it to a class. Which is why it's helpful to become buddies with at least one person in every class. Exchange phone numbers so they can clue you in on what you missed, and share notes and other important info. Of course, you will also do the same for your class buddy, so it's a win-win system.

Beyond that though, it's nice to have someone who's on your "team," so to speak. You can put your heads together for a homework assignment and exchange viewpoints on material. Plus, if you have the same major, you'll probably be seeing a lot of each other over the course of your college career. Who knows, this could be the start of a friendship that extends beyond graduation.

Develop a Mentor Relationship with an Upperclassman

Seek out upperclassmen who are on the same degree path or in the same department as you. They'll be your number one asset in doing well in difficult classes, anticipating what to expect with different professors, and finding out all the best college hacks. As an added bonus, it's a great way to avoid paying full price for textbooks. Upperclassmen will typically sell their old textbooks for a reduced amount to a fellow student.

Upperclassmen might seem a little intimidating at first, but remember that they're students, just like you. They were underclassmen once; they know what it's like. Strike up a conversation during one of your classes, get to know a student leader in a club or organization, or sign up for your school's peer mentor program to make a connection. You'll feel a lot less lost if you have a mentor to take you under their wing.

Establish a Strong Relationship with a Professor

Your interactions with your college professors are going to be completely different than the ones you had with your high school teachers. Some may only be a few years older than you, hilariously informal at times, or just all-around more approachable.

Building a good relationship with a professor is not only an attainable goal but a prudent one as well. For one thing, a letter of recommendation from a professor with whom you've built rapport will be miles better than any generic one. A professor can also offer you valuable advice along the way to help you better navigate tricky assignments and courses.

Make a point to introduce yourself at the end of class on the first day and speak up when participation is encouraged. Also get to know your professors better with some one-on-one time by setting up a meeting once a semester to check in with how you're doing. In addition, you can drop by for office hours anytime you have a question, are feeling confused about the material, or simply want to pick their brain for advice on a degree path.

Map Out
Your Dream Job

What job do you want when you finish college? Maybe you won't know exactly what that is during your freshman year. By sophomore year you might have a better, but still vague, idea. But by your junior year, things should start becoming clear. Once senior year rolls around, decisions have to be made: Will you be applying to full-time jobs or internships, or will you be applying to grad school?

Your experiences in college will help you figure out what kind of career you want to pursue (and which careers you definitely *don't* want to pursue). If there isn't one specific job you have in mind, consider what classes you find yourself drawn to each semester. Which topics are super-interesting to you? Also think about your favorite pastimes and passions. What jobs might allow you to enjoy these hobbies regularly? Be sure to check out average salaries and factor in the kind of lifestyle you want to lead as well.

Once you have these questions answered, you'll be able to start making a concrete plan for getting that dream job. Talk to professors in that field, do your research online, and reach out to people you may know who have the job (or similar job) you've got your sights on to learn what steps are necessary—both now and after graduation.

Study in Different Locations to Find the Spots That Maximize Your Productivity

Sometimes it feels like half the battle of studying is just finding a comfortable place where you can get in "the zone." And try as you might, being productive in your dorm can be challenging. Roommates and friends are likely to come in and out during your studying, and if you read in bed, the end result is usually an impromptu nap. You won't always live on campus, but there will always be downtime between classes that you can use for studying and working on homework.

You may be the type of person who does best studying in a secluded window seat of a common area where it's most calm. Or you might find that you have improved focus at the student union or student lounge area where there's a bit more background noise and it's easy to take breaks. Then again, it might depend on what type of material you're studying or even what kind of headspace you're in on any given day.

Research has shown that students who study in various locations retain information slightly better than students who always study in the same location. So spend some time finding two to three inviting study spots you can rotate through every week. You have access to all the dorms and other buildings—make the most out of exploring them!

Spend Time with a Therapy Dog (or Pig or Pony) During Finals Week

Unfortunately, you usually can't bring a pet with you to college. But on the bright side, more and more colleges are adopting pet therapy programs. Therapy animals, like friendly golden retrievers and cuddly rabbits, can help ease feelings of loneliness and homesickness you may have—especially if you're missing a pet back home.

In addition, animal-assisted therapy has been shown to be extremely effective at reducing stress and lowering anxiety. Taking a short break to pet or play with a dog can quickly enhance your mood. Additionally, interacting with a therapy animal has also been shown to improve clarity and focus. All of which is much needed during finals week!

You may find volunteers around campus (in the library for example) who allow you to "check out" the animal for a brief period of time, or one of the school counselors may have a therapy dog always available on campus. Get in touch with the mental health services at your school to get more information and find out about upcoming therapy animal events. Take advantage of this simple but effective way to manage stress—the service is free after all.

Sit in the Front Row of a Class for an Entire Semester

Make yourself sit in the front row of a lecture or class as a little experiment. Most students find that when they're "under surveillance" from the professor, they're more motivated to pay attention and be involved. Being noticed by your professor has the added benefit of fostering familiarity as well. And in a class where a lecture drones on, this little trick can help you stay just alert enough to resist falling asleep.

This experiment may just result in better grades, and who doesn't want that? Give it a shot for the next semester.

Complete a Big Project That You're Actually Proud Of

There will be countless class assignments and papers that you'll go through the motions to finish. And there's nothing wrong with that; if you're getting a passing grade, you're doing great! But you'll be doing yourself a disservice if you don't go all in on at least one project.

When the right free-form assignment comes along, channel some passion into it and turn it into something you can't wait to show off! It feels good to pour your heart into a project and end up with a great product worth sharing. Plus, learning how to cultivate passion in unlikely places is a skill that will serve you well, not only in your future career, but in all areas of your life! If you find yourself looking forward to spending time on the project, you know you're on the right track.

Apply for a Scholarship

Winning a scholarship is a nice goal to set for yourself because the reward is free money to pay for some of your college costs. It's also a really big confidence booster to see the results of your persistence pay off! And if someone else wins it this time, you can still feel proud knowing you put in a lot of effort and took a chance on something. You'll get 'em next time!

Before you jump into the process, be sure to check out tips online for applying, as well as common mistakes to avoid. Then look for scholarships that are a good fit for you (you can search by deadline month, your specific degree field, and qualities that make you unique) and check your school's website for any special awards they offer. Talk to your academic advisor, too, as they are usually in the loop about lesser-known scholarships.

Become a Teaching Assistant for a Favorite Class

Being a teaching assistant (TA) can be challenging at times, but it's also a super-rewarding opportunity. Not everyone gets to have the experience of TA-ing; it's similar to on-the-job experience, which means you'll gain a distinctive edge in the job market. Holding this position also helps you develop strong leadership skills and the ability to more efficiently manage your time. Another perk is a solid relationship with your professor that could lead to an excellent letter of recommendation—in addition to sage advice and valuable future connections. Some schools even pay TAs an hourly wage or reward them with financial tuition assistance—another win for you!

If you want to be an undergraduate teaching assistant, talk to your professor. Express your interest and ask about the requirements. Typically, you'll need to have done well in the particular class, and there may or may not be some training involved.

Form a Tight-Knit Study Group

Investing time in a study group is worthwhile even if you often find yourself taking the lead because you may learn more yourself just from helping your classmates. In fact, according to research, teaching others is one of the most effective ways to learn a subject. There will likely be areas when you're the one who could use a little help too. As you learn how to work as a team, it all balances out.

The trick to getting the most out of a study group is to study by yourself *first*. Everyone has a different pace and way they go about absorbing information. Plus, it's counterproductive to put your heads together before anyone has made an effort to understand the assignment or subject matter. Familiarize yourself with the content ahead of time so you can identify your personal strengths and weaknesses. After you've taken the time to review the material in the way that works best for you, focus on addressing the more challenging parts with your chosen classmates. Also let them know which areas you feel you understand really well so they can seek out your help if they are less confident in those parts of the assignment/subject matter.

The other big factor for forming a successful study group is finding other students who are serious about doing work. A study group feels like a waste of time when it turns into a social hour every time you meet up, right? Choose your study buddies wisely. Office hours are a great place to find and link up with some of your more studious classmates.

Get an A in a Hard Class

Getting good grades is, of course, fantastic for your GPA, but your GPA isn't the end-all, be-all of your existence in college. The bigger reason to get an A in a challenging class is to prove to yourself that you *can* do difficult things. Achieving this goal gives you a deeper sense of confidence in your own abilities. And with that confidence comes the motivation needed to follow through on pursuing what you really want in life.

Some tips for getting that *A*:

- Prioritize difficult classes over easier ones and budget your time accordingly

- Limit distractions when you're studying (e.g., phone notifications)

- Don't pass up opportunities for extra credit

- Handwrite your notes to retain information better

- Complete the required reading before lectures

Every little challenge you overcome puts you on the path to accomplishing things you may have never imagined possible for yourself. Receiving an *A* means moving one step closer to the life you want to live. Never underestimate the power of what you can do when you put your mind to it!

Up Your Typing Speed

From sending texts and emails to writing papers, typing is something you do every day and will likely continue to do for the foreseeable future. The main benefit of being able to type quickly and accurately is that it saves you time. You can probably think of a thousand other things you'd rather be doing than struggling to get your fingers to keep up with the speed of your thoughts.

If you learned the proper typing form back in grade school, you're one of the lucky ones; many students were never taught it. If not, no worries: Whether you have that preparation or not, with practice you can become proficient at typing. Start by reading some general tips online on how to increase your typing speed; these will cover the correct posture and where to place your fingers on the keyboard. Next, practice, practice, practice. You'll have plenty of opportunities to do so at college! There are also free typing exercises and tests you can try online, or there may even be a class offered on your campus.

When you improve your typing speed, you improve your productivity. Taking the time to work on this skill will make your life easier in the long run. Plus, being able to churn out a high number of words per minute will make you even more desirable in the job market after graduation.

Participate in
a UROP

UROP stands for Undergraduate Research Opportunities Program. If you have the chance to get in on research being conducted at your school, don't hesitate to seize it! Everyone has a small part of themselves that wants to change the world. Being involved with a UROP could be how you do that, because within research there are tons of opportunities to make a difference.

A UROP also makes sense for your future career as well. All of your peers who graduate with the same degree will become your job competition. Getting a jump on relevant experiences will help you distinguish yourself from everyone else.

To find an awesome UROP:

- Talk to your professors, TAs, advisor, organization leaders, and other students
- Look on your school's website
- Search online for research job postings

There are research programs out there for all academic disciplines. Don't let what might be a once-in-a-lifetime opportunity pass you by!

Challenge Yourself to Ask Ten Questions per Semester

Raising your hand in a lecture hall with hundreds of other students takes guts. Speaking in front of people, in general, can be scary, but once you push past your feelings of nervousness, it quickly becomes easier and easier.

Asking questions will help you get the most out of your classes. If you're thinking about it, a lot of your classmates probably are too. And honestly, long lectures are much more bearable when students are engaged and participating.

Challenge yourself to raise your hand at least ten times each semester (in every class, if you're feeling even more daring) and see what changes! You may just gain increased confidence and an improved learning experience. Plus, you can have a reward waiting for yourself once you hit ten questions. Treat yourself to anything from a fancier item on your favorite coffee shop's menu to a new shirt.

Join a Professional Organization in Your Field

Joining a professional organization related to your major can expose you to a whole host of prospects you may not find elsewhere. Benefits include learning about unique views and ideas within your field, as well as cutting-edge developments on the horizon. These organizations can also provide you with hands-on experience that will help you gain a better understanding of what it's like to work in your industry. The networking opportunities can be extremely helpful too!

Do an online search for "(your major)+professional organization" and talk to campus faculty to find one near you. Not all professional organizations are created equal, so be choosy about the one you join!

Convince Your Professor to Teach Outside on a Sunny Day

There will be days when the weather outside is calling your name and you'd much rather be enjoying it than sitting inside a lecture hall. Luckily, if you can convince your professor to move the class outside, you'll have a happy medium! College professors are often pretty laid-back, so it shouldn't take much to persuade one to go along with your idea—especially if your classmates are in on it too. It's fun to get a break from the classroom, and a change of scenery can actually make you and the other students *more* engaged in class.

Construct a convincing argument on why having class outside that day would enhance everyone's learning experience. Perhaps you have a presentation that you need to give outside to fully illustrate a concept, or maybe part of the lesson could use a real-world example. As a last resort, try telling your professor there are cookies in it for them.

Bring Treats
for the Whole Class

Remember how awesome it was to celebrate birthdays in grade school? Everyone was stoked because the birthday kid would usually bring in a special treat to share with the whole class. Despite a change in location and everyone being a bit older, you can still share in that excitement to a college class.

And you don't need to wait for your birthday to test this theory, either. Pick up a bulk tray of cookies from a warehouse club, snag some doughnuts from Krispy Kreme on $2 a dozen day, or bake some muffins if you have access to a kitchen. Bring in treats to one of your smaller classes for no particular reason other than to break up the midweek slump. You're sure to be the most popular student in class that day and may even inspire others to follow your lead!

Perform a Social Experiment

In the research world, a social experiment is used to gain insights into how people's behaviors and reactions are influenced by outward social pressures. That may sound a bit complicated, but it can actually be simple to try out for yourself.

Here are a few examples of social tests you can perform, no lab coat needed:

- Stand in front of a busy academic building, look up, and observe the ensuing confusion around you. People passing by will reflexively look up in the same direction or may even stop to try to figure out what you're looking at.

- Face away from the door when riding in an elevator. Get a few friends to do it with you and see what happens.

- Find out if you can successfully start a slow clap. Get a few friends in on the plan and have them spread throughout the class. When you start to clap, they can join in and everyone else might as well.

- Inconspicuously replace yourself with a cardboard cutout in a large lecture hall and time how long it takes before anyone notices.

A college campus is full of readily available test subjects, so in the name of science (or just fun), carry out an experiment of your own! It's an excellent way to kill downtime in between classes, satisfy your sense of curiosity, or simply goof around with friends. As you observe others, you may even be inspired to question and examine your own behaviors more closely.

Sign Up for a Bizarre Fitness Class

Whether you need to fill a prerequisite or just have a free hour to kill every Thursday, an unusual class can prove to be quite entertaining. After all, why take a run-of-the-mill cardio lab when you could be learning the art of Japanese swordsmanship? Other unique options might involve having a blast bouncing on trampolines, practicing your wakeboarding skills, recreational tree climbing, or even circus-related activities like juggling and walking a tightrope. Check out what your school has to offer, sign up for the most bizarre class you find, and enjoy college for the delightfully strange place that it can be!

Compile a List of a Professor's Most Quotable Moments

College professors say the darndest things. And they often don't even realize it. So it's up to you to capture and preserve these nuggets of comedy gold lest they be lost forever!

Start a text document to write down funny things a professor says during class. Note the date for each quote too. (Your professor probably won't remember uttering some—if not most—of these things, but the time frame could help jog their memory.) Compile your favorite quotes and then present them to your professor at the end of the semester. They're sure to get a kick out of it!

It's a fun side project to work on from start to finish, and you could even invite your classmates to join in. You may start looking forward to a class you used to dread or discover a new catchphrase in the process. Be sure to save a copy for yourself: It'll be a great way to relive some of the more hilarious parts of your college experience.

Complete an Online Certificate

College is a time when you're broadening your knowledge and widening your skill set. And your opportunities for learning aren't restricted to just a classroom setting. Online courses are convenient, and there are a myriad of topics and skills that you can get certified on. With a quick course, you could become an ordained minister, a notary (notarizing documents is a super-easy side hustle), or even a Jedi Knight.

Other online courses include training and certification for:

- Digital marketing
- Storm spotting
- Computer programing
- FEMA emergency management
- Dinosaur paleobiology

Whether you want to learn new skills to make extra money, become a more competitive job applicant, or have a cool certificate to hang on the wall, it's worth checking what's available online. Start your search by visiting OpenCulture.com, where you'll find a list of 1,500 free courses!

Create Your Own Bucket List

- [ ] _____
- [ ] _____
- [ ] _____
- [ ] _____
- [ ] _____
- [ ] _____
- [ ] _____
- [ ] _____
- [ ] _____
- [ ] _____
- [ ] _____
- [ ] _____
- [ ] _____
- [ ] _____
- [ ] _____
- [ ] _____
- [ ] _____

- [ ] _____
- [ ] _____
- [ ] _____
- [ ] _____
- [ ] _____
- [ ] _____
- [ ] _____
- [ ] _____
- [ ] _____
- [ ] _____
- [ ] _____
- [ ] _____
- [ ] _____
- [ ] _____
- [ ] _____
- [ ] _____
- [ ] _____
- [ ] _____
- [ ] _____
- [ ] _____

CHAPTER 5

Cultivating Your Best Self

College is a clean slate. No one remembers the embarrassing things you did in high school, nor cares whether you had a perfect GPA or barely passed calculus. The playing field has been leveled, so there's no need to let past years define you. With that in mind, what steps can you take now to become the person you've always wanted to be? And if you're satisfied with your path thus far, how might you continue to improve? Being your best self is about answering these questions and taking ownership of your life. And who you are—what that best self looks like—isn't concrete, either. It's something that will continue to evolve as you learn more about yourself through trying new things, accomplishing goals, and experiencing different highs and lows.

In this chapter, you'll discover dozens of ideas for progressing your sense of self through personal development. From life skills to treating your body with kindness to stimulating your mind and standing up for your emotional needs, these activities will help you uncover and expand your definition of *you*.

Become a Rock Star at Advocating for Yourself

Advocating for yourself means taking charge of your own life; it's about asking for what you need and making sure those needs are met.

As an adult journeying out on your own in college (and beyond), you need to be the one figuring out things like housing, financial aid, and grades. After all, nothing discredits your adulthood faster than having someone else fight your battles.

If you don't know exactly how to do all the adulting things yet, that's okay! A lot of the time it takes just a few seconds of bravery, and it'll get easier with practice. College is the perfect time to get a handle on self-advocacy: There are tons of opportunities to speak up for yourself, and mistakes are an expected part of the experience. And if you do need a little help along the way, that's okay too! Advocating for yourself also means asking for some guidance when you're feeling stuck or unsure of what to do.

Master the Art of Sewing On a Button

It's not hard to learn, but it's a skill that will come in handy for the rest of your life. Instead of having to buy new items, you might actually be able to fix the ones you have!

You can get a basic sewing kit pretty inexpensively that often includes one or two needles, a few spools of thread in different colors, and a simple needle threader. The actual steps are pretty simple, but you might find it takes some practice to get everything looking perfect: Check out some online tutorials for a visual guide.

You'll quickly develop a reputation for your abilities. Soon people you've never even met may be dropping off clothing for a quick mend.

Get a Reading from a Fortune-Teller

Now, while you're still figuring out who you are and what you believe in, is an excellent time to open yourself up to new experiences. Change is always hard and it only gets more difficult as you age. Choosing to be open (even to things that may seem silly from your perspective) instead of closed off is an exercise that will help you develop both your character and approach to life.

It's essential to challenge your assumptions and worldviews to grow as a person. Maybe your initial impressions about psychic readings, for example, aren't too far off the mark. But maybe having your fortune read will inspire you to do some research on the origins and you'll discover a new interest in the history of fortune-telling or similar practice.

Take a Picture of Yourself Every Day to Create a Time-Lapse Video

Imagine having a picture of yourself for every day in a whole year (or two or four years even). From one day to the next, you might not notice the gradual changes in your physical appearance. But when you get to watch yourself grow over the course of a year or more, the changes are a lot easier to spot. For one thing, those trends you thought were so cool as a freshman will probably make you laugh by the time you graduate. It's like a photographic diary you get to flip through whenever you want!

To create your own time-lapse video, you only need a camera (the one on your smartphone is more than adequate) and, of course, yourself. Or you can use a time-lapse app. Then, start snapping a picture of yourself once a day. The result is a priceless documentation of your college years that will always stir up memories.

Change a Tire Like a Pro

Flat tires happen from time to time, and they're never convenient. Knowing how to change a tire will not only make you more self-reliant (a great confidence booster!), but also save you time and money. When you possess the know-how, you won't have to call for roadside assistance or risk driving on a flat tire, which is not only dangerous, but can also damage the rim and cost you more in repairs.

Most cars already have everything you need to make the swap, including a:

- Spare tire (if it's not under the mat in the trunk, it could be on the underside of the car)

- Lug wrench

- Car jack

Verify all these items are in the trunk of your car and, if not, make sure to get them as soon as possible.

After pulling off to a safe location and turning on your hazard lights, the basic procedure to change your tire is as follows:

1. Set the parking brake.

2. Use the wrench to loosen, but do not remove, the lug nuts (turning counterclockwise).

3. Use the jack to lift the car. Locate the jack point (usually just behind the front and just before the rear wheels), place the jack underneath this point, and raise the car high enough for the wheel to spin freely.

4. Finish unscrewing the lug nuts.

5. Remove the flat tire and replace it with the spare.

6. Screw the lug nuts back on (leaving some room to tighten them in the next step).

7. Use the jack to lower the car all the way, then tighten the lug nuts (a quarter turn past snug should be good).

8. Head to the nearest tire dealer for a new tire.

Watch a *YouTube* video, reference your car's user manual, or better yet, ask a mechanically inclined family member or friend to walk you through the process for further instruction.

Perform
On Stage

As scary as they can seem, taking risks is part of growing as a person. You face your fears and build a sense of self-empowerment that will help you succeed through every part of life. Plus, taking chances can also reveal new possibilities you haven't considered before. College is the perfect time to test the waters and figure out what your limits truly are, as the opportunities to get out of your comfort zone are everywhere.

Find an introduction to improv class and be part of an improv show. Work out a comedy bit or try your hand at slam poetry. Audition for a part in an upcoming school play. The process of putting yourself out there and seeing just what you are capable of can lead to major gains in self-confidence!

Register to Vote Before the Next Presidential Election

On average, about 50 percent of the US population votes. If all the people who said their vote didn't matter *did* vote, it would make a difference! You may not be the deciding factor in an election, but you're contributing to a much more powerful whole.

Think of not voting as detracting from your side and strengthening the other. Why bother to complain about something on which you stayed silent? It's time to give your views a voice! Look up the requirements for your area to find out how to register; you can do it online in most states.

Plan Your Dream Trip

Right now, you might not be able to afford to spend a semester abroad and you might be so broke that traveling is beyond the realm of possibility, but who knows what unexpected opportunities will pop up in your future.

Planning is the first step to turning your dreams into reality. Think about a trip you'd love to take. Don't be afraid to dream big. Once you have the perfect destination in mind, you can calculate the estimated costs and even create a savings plan. After crunching numbers, you may discover that your dream trip isn't so out of reach after all when you break it down into manageable monthly savings goals.

Find a Sunscreen You Absolutely Love and Use It Daily

Lots of moisturizers, creams, and serums claim to be the best anti-aging product out there. But I'll let you in on a little secret: Sunscreen is the *actual* ultimate weapon for keeping your skin healthy and youthful. You may not be remotely concerned about wrinkles or skin discoloration at this stage in your life, but trust me, your future self will thank you for starting early!

Even if you couldn't care less about little imperfections, the biggest reason to wear sunscreen is to protect yourself from harmful UV rays that can lead to skin cancer—one of the top five most commonly occurring cancers out there.

Thankfully, there are options that will protect you without feeling gross on your skin or giving it that classic sunscreen smell. It's all about finding your personal holy grail. Because incorporating it into your daily routine *shouldn't* be something you dread.

To protect yourself from UVB and UVA rays, look for a sunscreen that has a rating of SPF 30 or higher, as well as a PPD 8+ or PA+++ rating. Do some research online to find a good fit for you. And if you don't love the first one you pick, try out more options until you do! It's life-changing when you find a sunscreen that feels exactly like a moisturizer and makes your skin happy.

Immerse Yourself In a Guided Meditation Group

Meditation is more than just a popular trend: It has benefits that are actually backed by science. It can reduce stress, lower anxiety, increase your attention span, and improve the quality of your sleep—all things that will take your college experience to the next level.

The problem is that most people never try meditation because they struggle with the concept. But here's the thing: The goal of meditation *isn't* to think about nothing. Very few can do that. In truth, there are a variety of styles and ways to meditate—none of which are necessarily better than another. The important thing is that you leave a meditation practice feeling satisfied.

As a beginner, you might find it helpful to go to a guided meditation group. In these groups, one person will explain the approach and then talk everyone through the practice in unison. You can find free groups to join locally on *MeetUp* or *Facebook*. Meditating as part of a group can help motivate you to actually do the practice, but it also has a certain *je ne sais quoi*. It's a feeling of connection that you have to experience firsthand to really understand.

If meditating as a group isn't your thing but you enjoy the guided part, look for guided sessions on *YouTube* or your favorite music streaming app. Aim to make your favorite meditation practice part of your daily routine.

Fall in Love with a Fitness Routine— and Stick To It

Building new habits only gets harder as you age, which is why it's so important to create good ones while you're in college. Creating habits around physical exercise is especially important, as it has a lot of worthwhile benefits, like:

- A release of feel-good endorphins that boost your mood
- An increase in brain function and thinking skills
- Improved sleep quality
- Increased productivity
- Increased energy levels
- A boost in your body's immunity

Truth be told, working out really doesn't take *that* much time. You can fit in a regular thirty-minute workout before breakfast, after your last class of the day, or even while studying with your notes on the treadmill. Convincing yourself to exercise when you'd rather just sleep in a little longer or lounge in the common room is a whole other story, of course. Getting started is the hardest part, but once you get into a routine, working out will become less of a chore—and maybe even something you look forward to.

Find a type of exercise you enjoy (or at least don't completely hate) and start taking advantage of the student fitness center every week—it's *free*, after all. To stay motivated you can try using a habit tracker, having an accountability buddy, visualizing your success, and rewarding yourself for reaching both small and large goals. You'll be doing not only your current self a huge favor, but your future self a favor as well!

Grow a Plant from a Seed

Watching a full, flourishing plant grow from a tiny seed is a fun and beautiful process. It teaches you lessons about the value of patience and how rewarding responsibility can be. You'll start with a seemingly lifeless speck, and by the time it's a thriving, leafy thing, you'll have a sense of parental pride over it.

There is a "risk" you'll develop an obsession with gardening. But as far as hobbies go, this one lets you get your fix for cheap. You may even end up with herbs or vegetables you can eat! Do a little research online for information on which plants are best for beginners to get started.

Visit a Museum for Free with Your Student ID

With a little help from your student ID, you can get free (or at least discounted) access to museums and other cultural institutions. Seize the opportunity to see what these local, illuminating locations have to offer! Some of the greatest human achievements can be found within their walls.

Whether you're a fine arts aficionado, history buff, or just looking for a new way to kill an afternoon, you're likely to find inspiration in some form. You'll discover a sea of thought-provoking gallery pieces, insights into different parts of history, or maybe even a new passion. Appreciate just letting yourself absorb the sights—and the feelings they stir up.

Take a Pre-Dawn Hike to Watch the Sunrise

Gain a deeper appreciation for nature and harness its revitalizing power. Making a point to get away from it all every now and then will help you clear your mind of the clutter of homework, roommate problems, weekend plans, and more. An early-morning hike also has a few key differences that make it stand out compared to a mid-day or evening hike. Cool, crisp air in your lungs, and a quiet, empty trail set a peaceful mood that you'll carry with you for the rest of the day. And of course, watching the sunrise is a stunning sight in itself.

Top off your little adventure with a satisfying breakfast and you've got yourself a perfect morning!

Be Able to Do
at Least One Pull-Up

The ability to perform one *real* pull-up escapes even those of us who are relatively fit. It's a true test of functional strength. You can get there, but patience is key.

Start by practicing negative hangs every day: Use a chair or jump up to bring your chin above the bar, lower yourself as slowly as possible, and then repeat. You can do these on a doorway pull-up bar, a playground, or even a sturdy tree branch. Increase the amount of repetitions you do over time and do static holds before slowly lowering yourself to increase your strength. (Check out a video or two on *YouTube* for visual instructions.)

When the day comes that you can finally do a full pull-up, you'll feel like a total badass. Do it for the bragging rights, in case you ever need to haul yourself up over something, or do it just for the sake of challenging yourself.

Read One Book Recreationally Each Semester

Every semester, make a point to read at least one thing besides your textbooks and other assigned books. Why? According to mountains of research, reading for fun makes you a better student. It can aid in keeping your mental abilities sharp, expand your vocabulary, broaden your knowledge, and improve your critical thinking skills. Plus, regularly reading for pleasure is associated with lower levels of stress and depression.

Many students who were avid readers in high school find themselves not reading as much in college. It's easy to let the habit fall by the wayside when you have so many other things going on! However, it's worthwhile to cultivate, or reignite, a love of books during your college years. Reading is one of the least expensive hobbies you can get into, and the possibilities for stimulating the imagination are endless.

There are tons of books to choose from, and more are published every year. From romance and mystery to fantasy and memoirs, you're sure to find at least a few titles that pique your interest. And remember: You have an entire library available to you right at your school. If you have no idea where to even begin, ask the librarian or your friends for recommendations!

Take a
Self-Defense Class

Beyond protecting yourself, the benefits of learning self-defense include increased self-confidence, feelings of security, speedier reaction times, and improved physical fitness. These classes stress preparing you to handle any circumstances where there is the potential for harm. In addition to physical defense techniques, you can also learn how to stay vigilant and avoid risky situations whenever possible. You'll essentially be learning street smarts (which are very different from book smarts).

Police departments, colleges, and other institutions frequently offer self-defense classes for free, so you really have no reason to miss out. Plus, taking a course could awaken something inside of you that you otherwise would have never known was there. You may uncover a newfound passion for contact sports like mixed martial arts, find that punching and kicking things is an excellent de-stresser (hello, kickboxing), or realize that this was just the thing you needed to further develop your self-discipline skills.

Create a Personalized Self-Care Routine

The fastest way to end up burnt out in college is to never set aside time for yourself. It's easy to neglect your physical and mental needs when it seems like you have one thousand other things to do. And feeling like you always need to be busy doesn't stop after you graduate. In fact, the need to always be on the go and doing, well, anything, may intensify.

However, there is a lot more to life than getting things done, and one of the most important of these is self-care. Self-care is any act that makes you feel better, whether physically, mentally, or spiritually. You can't pour from an empty cup, and self-care is all about carving out time for the things that will leave you feeling recharged, refreshed, and ready for whatever lies ahead.

Simple self-care activities include:

- Starting the day with yoga
- Going out for ice cream after a tough exam
- Relaxing in nature
- Listening to your favorite music
- Giving yourself a face, hand, or foot massage

Making self-care a priority will help you handle everything that's being thrown at you during college—and beyond. There is no one-size-fits-all definition for self-care, either, so experiment to find the practices that are right for your needs.

Learn to Cook Something Beyond Instant Food

Ordering out all the time, though delicious and convenient, gets seriously expensive! Instant food goes hand-in-hand with college life because you can make it in a jiff when you're strapped for time (which is almost always). But after a while, you'll tire of ramen, pizza rolls, and pudding cups. You'll begin to have vivid dreams of home-cooked meals and you may find that your mouth waters when your mom mentions over text that she cooked her famous tater tot casserole for dinner the previous night.

Maybe you'll be rich enough to afford a personal chef in the future, but in the meantime, being able to cook a few meals without setting off the smoke alarm is quite the useful skill. For one, throwing together the ingredients yourself will save you a ton of money. And for two, you'll have something to show off during a date.

Whether you have a shared kitchen or just a microwave at your disposal, there are tons of easy recipes you can master. Just hop online and start searching! Include terms like "easy," "simple," "microwave," and "for college students." If you're more of a visual learner, *YouTube* is an excellent place to find full recipe tutorials.

Become a Pro at Budgeting

The way you handle your money has a *huge* impact on your life during college—and forever after. It's best to educate yourself about handling finances now, before it gets more and more complicated as the different bills and other expenses are added to the equation.

While personal finance likely wasn't a part of your high school curriculum, you do have the opportunity to learn money management skills now by taking a personal finance class or doing research online.

The basic concept of budgeting is to live within your means and not spend money you don't have. To create a personalized budget:

1. Figure out the total amount of income you have going into your bank account on a weekly or monthly basis.

2. List all your expenses and total them up. Expenses can be both fixed (meaning the amount doesn't change, like your monthly phone bill) and flexible (meaning how much you spend isn't set in stone, i.e., groceries).

3. Subtract your expenses from your income and see what you're left with. For flexible expenses, estimate and average the amount to use in this equation.

4. If you have more expenses than income, consider how you can reduce costs or cut down on nonessential spending. The goal

is to have some money left over so you can spend it on things you want (or save it for a rainy day).

Use an app or printable worksheet (a quick search online will reveal tons of free ones) to keep your budget on track, but don't be too hard on yourself if things go a bit awry! Budgeting is a learning process, so give it some time and try different methods such as zero-based budgeting, the cash envelope system, or a pay-yourself-first budget. The most important part is that you reevaluate often, either monthly or weekly, and adjust what you're doing from there. With time and perseverance, you'll gain mastery over your budget, and with it, you'll be able to stress less about money and enjoy life more!

Take the Chance on a Blind Date or Speed-Dating Event

Dating in college can be exciting, confusing, and, at times, overwhelming. During your undergraduate career, you'll interact with a myriad of people—many of whom are interested in expanding their romantic life. And while there is no shortage of singles who're ready to mingle, putting yourself out there can be a bit nerve-racking.

Going on a blind date or two is a great way to get the ball rolling. You and your friends can play matchmaker for each other and go on double or group dates. You might have a great time, make a new friend, or maybe meet your soul mate. Even if a date could've gone smoother, you'll get a good story out of it!

Speed-dating events are also fun because they offer even more chances for connection. Look online for an event in your area (sometimes they happen on campus) and bring your single friends along. If nothing else, you'll walk away having increased your confidence, met a bunch of different people, and experienced something new.

Learn a Skill You Can Make Money with on the Side

Learning a new skill that you can use to make money, or banking on one you already possess, is a smart idea for any college student. It's always nice to have extra money for when you really want some easy, delicious takeout, or when you get invited on a weekend trip. Plus, knowing you don't need to rely on your degree alone gives you more security and flexibility once you've graduated. Say you're offered a job in a desirable location but the salary leaves something to be desired. With the extra padding from a side gig, you won't feel like you have to pass up on that great opportunity to live where you want to and grow in your chosen career. You also won't feel as pressured to grab any job offer that comes your way.

Here are some money-making ideas that might be a good fit for you:

- If you have a passion for fitness, sell custom gym routines, meal prepping plans, or one-on-one coaching sessions
- If you love thrifting, flip items you find at garage sales and consignment stores for a profit by listing them on *eBay*
- If you're good with animals, try specializing in dog training sessions, grooming, or pet sitting services, or become a pet butler (yes, it's a real gig!)
- If you're great at making cocktails, bartend weddings and small private events
- If you're into music, start a cover band and play gigs

Anything is possible! Go online to search for more ideas and get your creative juices flowing.

Set Strong Personal Boundaries—and Enforce Them

You've probably heard about personal boundaries before, but what are they exactly? Personal boundaries are guidelines you set for how the people in your life treat you. It's not about forcing someone to change (after all, the only person you can control is yourself); it's about communicating clearly about what you will not tolerate in a relationship and how you react if/when a person crosses a line.

Establishing healthy boundaries is a big part of valuing your own needs and wants. Doing so actually encourages others to respect you more, because you have boundaries—and stick to them—rather than let others walk all over you.

The first step to setting personal boundaries is thinking about your limits. Create a list of what behaviors you find unacceptable. If you are having trouble making your list, think back to past experiences where someone said or did something that made you feel uncomfortable or even in danger. These are boundaries.

Once decided, you'll need to communicate your boundaries to those around you and enforce them by speaking up if someone steps over them. For example, if your friend asks you about a sensitive subject, tell them you aren't comfortable talking about it. If they don't respect your boundary and keep asking, remove yourself from the situation. And if that still doesn't get the message across, you may need to reevaluate the relationship as a whole.

As you practice being assertive about your needs, you will likely find a deeper sense of self-worth, experience more fulfilling relationships, and become happier overall. Enforcing your boundaries may feel awkward or unnatural at first, but it's crucial for your mental health.

Write Three Sentences Every Day

Start a journal with a notebook, an app on your phone, or a simple, text-based document in your computer. Then, set the goal to write something in your journal every day. Some days you may have more to write than others, but three sentences is a good minimum amount. You can remind yourself to write by adding a recurring note in your phone calendar.

Writing even just a little bit every day is an amazing tool for self-reflection. Long after you've graduated from college you'll be able to read what you wrote and remember the experiences more clearly than if you relied on your memories alone. It really is fascinating to see yourself grow and change over the years! And in the specific moment, writing can be a cathartic release when you're stuck in negative emotions or facing a difficult situation. It helps to get out all the thoughts and feelings swirling around inside so you can move forward with a calm, clear mindset.

Teach a Class in Something You Love

You could instruct swim lessons, coach a youth sports team, or lead a knitting class at a community center. Just be the one teaching for a change! Teaching any type of class is a valuable experience because it gives you a new perspective on things and prepares you for life in the working world.

Teaching can help you develop your capacity for patience, challenge your problem-solving skills, and expand your ability to communicate clearly (especially if you're teaching young kids). Plus, it's a nice way to make money! You'll meet new people who you may become good friends with. And, of course, you'll have fun—it might even be an undiscovered passion!

Get Comfortable Doing Things Alone

Is there a café you want to go to but all your friends are busy? Go alone and enjoy that Danish you've been craving all day. You may bump into someone you know (or a friendly stranger) and have a captivating conversation. Or you may have a peaceful afternoon to yourself.

As wonderful as spending time with others can be, alone time can be just as beneficial. From grocery store trips to doctor visits to seeing a movie no one you know is interested in, being alone is a situation you'll encounter countless times in your life. And the more you're okay with doing things unaccompanied, the more confidence you'll gain. Getting comfortable with solitude early by practicing it during college will also save you from a lot of unneeded anxiety and stress down the line.

As you grow bolder, you may find yourself less likely to let amazing opportunities pass you by out of the fear of being alone—and a happier person for it.

Create Your Own Bucket List

- [ ] _____
- [ ] _____
- [ ] _____
- [ ] _____
- [ ] _____
- [ ] _____
- [ ] _____
- [ ] _____
- [ ] _____
- [ ] _____
- [ ] _____
- [ ] _____
- [ ] _____
- [ ] _____
- [ ] _____
- [ ] _____
- [ ] _____
- [ ] _____

- [ ] _____
- [ ] _____
- [ ] _____
- [ ] _____
- [ ] _____
- [ ] _____
- [ ] _____
- [ ] _____
- [ ] _____
- [ ] _____
- [ ] _____
- [ ] _____
- [ ] _____
- [ ] _____
- [ ] _____
- [ ] _____
- [ ] _____
- [ ] _____
- [ ] _____
- [ ] _____

CHAPTER 6

Creating Good Karma

No matter what your beliefs may be, the consensus is that if everyone was nice to one another and the environment, the world would be a better place. Sometimes it can be hard to have empathy, though—especially when you're busy with homework, plans with friends, sports practice, and more. But like a muscle, cultivating good karma is something you have to work at regularly for it to grow and strengthen. And why does good karma matter? For one thing, committing little acts of kindness makes you feel good inside. More importantly, it's being the change you want to see in the world. You have the ability to put good vibes out into the universe one small good deed at a time.

This chapter offers creative ways for you to practice the golden rule of treating others as you want to be treated. You'll explore ideas for spreading kindness on your campus, thoughtful things to do for your loved ones, tips for brightening a random stranger's day, and simple, yet impactful actions for cultivating a positive mindset in your everyday life.

Surprise a Loved One with a Visit Home

The best gift you can give a close family member is quality time with you. Being away at college can really help you appreciate all the things they used to do for you—and the things you used to do together. Take this opportunity to thank them for all those years of laundry folding, delicious dinners, or helping you learn the self-sufficiency skills you need to succeed on your own. You might even consider returning the favor by picking up a few chores to help them out while you're home!

Pay for the Order Behind You at the Dining Hall

It's a simple gesture that will come as a complete surprise to a stranger and brighten their day. Finding out someone paid for your order puts a special little twist on an everyday situation like grabbing lunch between classes. If you're not too strapped for cash—or have extra swipes on your dining hall card you likely won't use—pay it forward (or in this case backward) with this random act of kindness. That person may even be inspired to try their own random act of kindness.

Participate in a Local Nature Cleanup

Helping with a local cleanup event for a beach or a park is an excellent way to volunteer your time. Not to mention, it can be quite the eye-opener. Even if you're aware of littering being a common problem, you might be shocked to see exactly how much trash your group can collect in just a few hours.

Participating in a cleanup can definitely shift your perspective on eco-friendly practices, as well as encourage you to be more conscious about how you dispose of your own trash. Every little bit helps, and it feels good to work with the power of a larger group to make a difference! There's no shortage of cleanup efforts; your school is sure to organize a few of their own. You can also search online to find upcoming events in the area.

Be an Enthusiastic Spectator for a Less Popular Club

Everyone goes to football games, but sports are far from the only competitive events going on at your school. Typically there are also debate team matches and meetups/competitions for other clubs like Quiz Bowl, Robotics, and Chess. However, these events often draw fewer crowds or are forgotten during sports games.

Be someone who shows up and roots these clubs on! It'll make those students' day, can be really interesting to watch, and who knows, you may discover a new favorite event to attend.

Be a Designated Driver for a Party

College is the time when a lot of people learn their limits with alcohol. And it is these situations where a little responsible planning can help prevent some very regrettable choices, like driving drunk. Most students going to a party won't want to be the designated driver, so you'll find that they're appreciative of you stepping up to task to ensure they get home safely.

Honestly, you don't need to drink to have fun at a party. You can still play all the games, swapping the alcohol with water, soda, or a caffeine beverage of your choice. Plus, socializing is arguably more entertaining when you have your wits about you. Best of all, you won't wake up with a hangover the next morning!

Leave Sticky Notes with Nice Messages in Library Books

The goal here is simple: Brighten a stranger's day just because! A sticky note with a positive message is a nice little surprise for the person who finds it. Though unexpected, a few words of encouragement can be remarkably meaningful.

This is a great activity to do sporadically during your time at college because you have a library full of books right on campus. And it's an easy act of kindness to carry out: Simply jot down a nice thought, a quote you love, or something someone once said to you that made you happy. Then choose a book at the library; it can be one of your favorite titles or any old random book. You might stick the note inside the front cover to be discovered right away, or somewhere within the pages for the reader to find later on.

You never know what kind of impact a small gesture can have. You may even start a chain reaction where more and more of your fellow students join in to leave notes!

Smile and Give a Thumbs-Up to a Classmate During Their Presentation

Giving a presentation to a full class is no simple feat—even for students who are more experienced with public speaking. Listening to class presentations can be dull and boring at times, and the other students (you included) may struggle to stay engaged. But everyone has to get up in front of the class at some point. Remember, you're all in this together and the golden rule (treat others the way you want to be treated) applies in this situation.

A crowd filled with students who are falling asleep, talking, or seem otherwise disinterested can be pretty disheartening. But a friendly face and a little support go a long way. So give a presenting classmate a smile and a thumbs-up. You'll be helping them feel more at ease and a little more confident. And maybe they'll return the favor for you in the future.

Attend a Bingo Night at an Assisted Living Facility

Visit a local assisted living or retirement home on bingo night and play a few rounds. Bingo is a social event, so don't be shy: Introduce yourself to the older attendees at your table. They'll love you for taking an interest in getting to know them; plus, you'll likely get to hear some great stories of yesteryear. You may be surprised at how fast the time flies even though you planned on only staying for an hour or two!

Transitioning to an assisted living or retirement community can be difficult, and some seniors may not see their family very often. Interactions with a spry college student such as yourself can help raise their spirits and ease some feelings of loneliness. Beyond bingo night, you can also talk to the staff to inquire about how to volunteer at the facility on a more regular basis. There might also be an "Adopt-a-Grandparent" club at your university you can tag along with.

Volunteer at an Animal Shelter when Puppy and Kitten Fever Strikes

Pets are almost always banned from the dorms, and even if you live in an apartment off campus, it's often too difficult to get an animal when you're constantly on the go. Puppy and kitten fever is *real* though, especially if you have family pets back home that you're missing. When you feel like you can't resist the temptation of a cute sidekick any longer, spend some time volunteering at an animal shelter. Getting your fill of cuddles while also refreshing your memory on how much responsibility it is to care for a pet can be just the cure for that fever.

Volunteers are always needed, so it shouldn't be difficult to find a local organization that's looking for helpers. You can call or search online to find out how to sign up. As a volunteer, you'll be working with animals who normally spend a lot of time in kennels and only get limited human interaction. From going on walks to giving baths and imparting unconditional love, any time you spend with them makes a world of difference to the critters who are waiting to be adopted.

Volunteering at an animal rescue can also help improve your own mood as well. You'll develop new skills, meet new people, gain a deeper sense of empathy, and make a real difference in the lives of animals. As you make new connections within the animal welfare community, you might even uncover an interest in a different career path!

Hide a Painted Rock
in a Local Park

The painted rock movement (sometimes referred to as "kindness rocks") is all about using art and creativity to brighten someone's day. With the help of local *Facebook* groups, it's also a popular game of hide-and-seek for kids. Each unique rock is like a bit of treasure for the child who's actively seeking, or pleasantly surprised by, it.

Taking part in this feel-good trend is as simple as gathering a few rocks, paints, and paintbrushes and letting your imagination run wild. It's an enjoyable group activity too, so bring your friends in on the project! You could paint superhero faces, mandalas, miniature landscapes, quotes, or whatever else your heart desires. If you're really feeling crafty, you can use polymer clay to take your designs to the next level; check out videos on *YouTube* for step-by-step instructions.

It's common to include instructions on the bottom of the rock encouraging the finder to share a picture to a *Facebook* group, but it's not absolutely necessary. You can also hide the rocks anywhere you like; a hiking trail, near a baseball field, or on a playground are all good spots. Finding a good place to hide the rock can be a fun challenge in itself!

When You See Something, Say Something

Be the person who speaks up when you see a situation where someone could get hurt, or something dangerous may be going on. Never assume that someone else will do something about it: When everyone is thinking that, *no one* takes action.

You don't need to insert yourself into a possibly risky situation, either. If you see something bad, or even questionable, unfolding, notify campus security, call 911, or get your RA. Become the person who does the right thing simply because it's the right thing to do.

Of course, it can be really hard to stand up in these situations, especially when no one else seems all that concerned. But if you're worried about being seen as a whistleblower, most of the time you can stay anonymous. At the end of the day, you'll always be proud of yourself for calling out unacceptable behavior.

Help a Stranger— and Never Tell Anyone about It

Nothing is loved more on social media than a feel-good story of service. But sometimes it's a wonder if people are doing these good deeds more for the kindness of it…or for the pat on the back. While that doesn't make helpful actions any less good, there's something extra special about performing a selfless act and telling no one about it.

Doing something just for the sake of kindness is authenticity in its purest form. A genuine desire to do good shifts the focus away from gaining the approval of others. It helps you stay grounded and become a more humble person. And college is the perfect time to work on instilling these valuable qualities.

Try it out the next time you have the opportunity to help someone in need. You're sure to feel good inside and may really enjoy having a happy little secret to keep all to yourself.

Do Something Not-So-Fun for Someone Else

What's a chore or activity that you absolutely loathe doing? Laundry? Cleaning? Mowing the lawn? Whatever it is, go do that thing in its entirety for someone else, whether a parent, grandparent, neighbor, or friend.

Do a really good job and remember you're doing this for someone else! After it's all said and done, it's likely you'll have a deeper appreciation for the people in your life. In addition, cultivating a thankful attitude will improve your relationships. Taking the time to appreciate the little things can also help you lead a happier life in general.

Bake Your Favorite Goodies and Share Them with Your Neighbors

Baking can be fun—both the process and the end result! But it's easy to get carried away when you want to make just a sampling of treats and each recipe yields way too much for just one person. You obviously can't let your baked goods go to waste, so why not share the wealth with your neighbors?

Whether you're living in a dorm or an apartment, it's a great excuse to get to know those living near you a little better. Your tasty creations are a guaranteed way to brighten their day (consider asking about any food allergies first). You may find out you have something in common, or even start a never-ending exchange of baked goods. In the end, it's a nice thing to do just because!

Fundraise for a Charity

College is a great time to get involved with a cause, as it's so common for clubs and organizations to put on fundraising events. Nonprofit groups put a lot of good out into the world, and fundraising helps support them in their goals. By fundraising, you can also help spread awareness for the charity of your choice, learn beneficial leadership skills, and connect with like-minded people.

You can volunteer at a charity event right on campus or find one taking place off campus. Get in contact with the director of Student Activities or Student Affairs, as they'll be the ones in charge of overseeing any fundraising events and should be able to point you in the right direction.

Gift a Family Member with a Re-Created Photo from Your Childhood

Re-creating a photo from your childhood can be quite the entertaining project to take on. The premise is simple: Choose a picture of yourself from when you were a kid, copy whatever you were doing and wearing, and then snap a new picture. So if you were decked out in a bright yellow romper while sitting in a little red wagon as a three-year-old, that means you'll be donning a bright yellow romper and squeezing into a little red wagon now as a twenty-one-year-old. As you can imagine, the results are hilarious and endearing at the same time.

Once you have the photo, hold onto it until the perfect occasion arrives. You'll be person of the year if you give it to a parent, grandparent, or other close family member on their birthday. They'll treasure the photo and the efforts you went through to take it more than anything you could ever buy. As a broke college student, that's a huge win!

Email or Write a Teacher Who Made a Difference in Your Life

Showing your appreciation is an easy way to make another person feel valued. Expressing it may not come to you naturally; however, it's an excellent habit to develop while you're young because a grateful outlook will benefit all relationships in your life—both business and personal. It feels nice when someone goes out of their way to thank you, right?

The goal of every teacher is to make a positive difference in their students' lives. Teaching can be discouraging sometimes, but an email or letter from a past student can make their efforts feel vindicated. So take some time to express your gratitude for all that they did for you. It doesn't take much to make someone else feel special, and you never know how well timed your note might be. It could be just the pick-me-up they needed after a lousy week!

Talk to a Loved One on the Phone Regularly

From *Facebook* and *Instagram* to voice notes and group chats, there's no shortage of ways to communicate in this digital age. Phones are hardly used for their original function and it's getting to the point where it feels foreign to call someone. But as cool, hip, and "with the times" as parents, aunts or uncles, or grandparents might be, talking on the phone is the mode of communication they value most (aside from seeing you in person, of course).

You'll make your loved ones *so* happy by simply calling to chat, and honestly, it takes such little effort on your part. Instead of ringing them only on holidays/special occasions, pick up the phone once a month and see how it improves both of your lives.

Remember your older relatives have been around the block a time or two, so they can be a wealth of wisdom. From family history to relationship advice and financial guidance, there's a lot you can learn from your family. Over time you may start to look forward to hearing their smile through the phone, become inspired by their stories of tenacity, or form a deeper bond. There's only so much time you can spend with your loved ones, so treasure them while you can!

Tape a Few Dollars to a Vending Machine on Campus

Have you ever been busy and *super*-hungry, silently wishing you could grab something to eat? Only you can't, because there isn't enough time to run to the dining hall or back to your room to grab some change for a snack from the vending machine. If only it would accept an IOU (you know you're good for it!).

It's not a fun experience—but it does present an easy way to show kindness to your fellow student. The next time you do have some money on you, tape a dollar or two to a vending machine (or leave quarters in the coin return) on campus so someone can enjoy a free snack. Finding quarters in a coin-operated machine was like finding treasure as a kid. Making such a discovery as a broke college student is arguably even better. No matter who finds what you left behind, you'll effectively be someone's snack guardian angel!

Befriend a Campus Staff Member and Have Lunch with Them

Chat up one of your school's staff members, such as a custodian, receptionist, cafeteria worker, or security guard, and make friends with them. These folks are frequently disregarded even though they work really hard to keep campuses clean and running smoothly. It doesn't take much to be nice and treat them with the respect they deserve. During a lunch together you may discover they're one of the coolest people in the school and become good pals.

Being nice to everyone, regardless of their rank and/or title, is a way of living that you can carry over to your future workplace and beyond. Being courteous and friendly will get you far! Not only is it the right way to treat others, but you'll also make numerous allies and forge valuable connections throughout every stage of your life.

Take Part in a Protest for Something You Believe In

From the Berkeley Free Speech Movement to the first Earth Day in 1970 to the Keystone XL Pipeline Protest at Georgetown University, student protests make history. You'll find social movements happening on college campuses all across the nation, so there's no time like now to get in on the action.

Protesting is not just one of your fundamental rights but also an essential part of a democratic society. Participating in activism for a cause you believe in will connect you with people who share your values. It's also an important way to highlight issues and have your voice be heard. With the power of mass mobilization on your side, you can direct your beliefs into action and be part of influencing change.

Before you take part in a protest, it's smart to know your rights well. Your right to free speech is protected by the First Amendment on public university grounds, but private institutions aren't as straightforward. Check your student handbook for rules on demonstrations and be sure to read safety tips online before jumping into action!

Help Someone with Car Troubles

If you've ever been stranded due to car troubles before, you know how frustrating it can be. Everyone does it at some point, but you can't help but feel at least a little bit embarrassed about accidentally killing your car battery by leaving the lights on. You probably also know what it's like to hope a helping hand will stop. Be that person.

You don't need to be a mechanic or even good with cars to help someone out of a jam. Sometimes it's nice to just have company while waiting for the tow truck to arrive. It's also easy to follow online instructions to help someone jump-start their car. (Not to mention it's a good idea to keep a set of jumper cables along with a roadside emergency kit in your car in case of an emergency just like this one.) When you're prepared, the opportunity to be a Good Samaritan will present itself—likely right in your school's parking lot!

Get In the Habit of Giving Out Compliments Like Candy

Everyone has a basic emotional need to be acknowledged and appreciated. Compliments address both; it always feels good to receive them. But meaningless and insincere flattery will get you nowhere: People are pretty good at seeing through it. Be specific and leave out "I" when giving a compliment because it keeps the focus on the other person and comes across as more sincere. For example, instead of saying, "I love your new glasses," go with, "Those glasses look great on you!"

Get in the habit of giving out compliments freely and frequently. Beyond making someone's day, observing and appreciating the good in people also has surprising benefits. You may notice you're becoming a more optimistic person, your relationships are taking a turn for the better, or you just feel happier in general.

Appreciate Five People by Snail Mail

Send letters to five people just letting them know you really appreciate them and why. It's less common for people to write letters nowadays, which is exactly why receiving one (especially out of the blue) is so special. A letter is more personable than a text or an email. It means the person who sent it went through extra steps, which makes the gesture feel more thoughtful.

Buy a pack of greeting cards and fill one out whenever you're feeling inspired. Or if you were gifted stationery that you never seem to have a use for, this activity is the perfect excuse to break it out. Sometimes it's difficult to know where to start or what to write, but keep in mind that your message doesn't need to be perfect or even that long to make the other person feel valued. Not only does a little recognition go a long way, but it is also key to sustaining long-lasting and meaningful relationships of all kinds.

Lend Someone Your Umbrella When It's Raining

When you're having a bad day, sometimes the best way to turn your mood around is to help someone who's having a worse day than yourself. Give it a shot when you see a fellow student caught in an unexpected downpour with a look on their face that signals *this is it; this is the straw that is going to break the camel's back today.* Cue you, the unexpected hero, swooping in to save the day with your umbrella. It's sure to bring a smile (no matter how brief) to the stranger's face in spite of the weather. As a consequence, you may begin to feel a break in the dark clouds of your own mood too.

It doesn't take grand gestures to restore someone's faith in humanity; it's the little things. Of course, while being considerate is a great quality, it does take conscious efforts to fully develop. Giving your umbrella to a stranger is one simple way to practice it. Plus, your kind act might even start a domino effect. How fun would it be to see dozens of other students sharing their umbrellas as well?

Introduce Yourself to Someone Sitting Alone in the Dining Hall and Eat with Them

Meeting people in the dorms is easy. Meeting new people in the dining hall is also easy, but, quite frankly, underrated. Introduce yourself to someone sitting alone in the cafeteria and ask if you can sit with them. It might be just what they needed to feel less lonely. Or maybe they are enjoying some alone time: It's still a great reminder that someone friendly is around if they do want company. You might just spark a great friendship. If nothing else, you'll have met someone new and maybe had an interesting conversation while eating your meal.

Pass Along Your College Wisdom to a Lowerclassman

Your junior or senior year is a great time to share some of your college wisdom. By this point in your college career, you're over halfway done and you've learned a lot along the way. You may have benefitted from a mentor-mentee type relationship with an upperclassman as a freshman student yourself. However, you don't need to have had that experience to make a great mentor now!

There are two main ways to link up with a lowerclassman looking for guidance:

1. Organically in a class or club, during an event, or through a mutual friend.

2. Through a freshman/first year mentor program where students are often matched by major and similar interests.

As a mentor, you'll essentially be helping a new student with the transition to college life. You can provide valuable insight about what to expect, since you've already gone through what they're now going through.

There's no one-size-fits-all approach for mentor relationships, so don't stress over trying to be perfect. Just do your best to be approachable, supportive, and someone they feel comfortable confiding in when they have a problem. It's an opportunity for you to share your best tips and tricks—anything you wish you'd known as a freshman. You may develop a long-lasting friendship, discover you really like being a mentor, or inspire your mentee to follow the same path when they're older!

Stop and Reflect Once a Week

The basic thought process behind karma is that what goes around comes around. In your quest for cultivating good energy, your thoughts go hand in hand with your actions. They shape your reality and how you handle what comes your way, so regularly connecting with your inner world is crucial for putting your best foot forward.

Take some time once a week to reflect on your recent experiences—both in how you've acted toward others and in what has happened generally. College goes by in a flash, especially when you're having fun! Setting aside time for introspection will help you relive highlight moments, improve upon an attitude of gratitude, and ponder any negative emotions that may have been stirred up in the past week so you can move toward healing.

Create Your Own Bucket List

- [ ] _____
- [ ] _____
- [ ] _____
- [ ] _____
- [ ] _____
- [ ] _____
- [ ] _____
- [ ] _____
- [ ] _____
- [ ] _____
- [ ] _____
- [ ] _____
- [ ] _____
- [ ] _____
- [ ] _____
- [ ] _____
- [ ] _____
- [ ] _____

- [ ] _____
- [ ] _____
- [ ] _____
- [ ] _____
- [ ] _____
- [ ] _____
- [ ] _____
- [ ] _____
- [ ] _____
- [ ] _____
- [ ] _____
- [ ] _____
- [ ] _____
- [ ] _____
- [ ] _____
- [ ] _____
- [ ] _____
- [ ] _____
- [ ] _____
- [ ] _____

CHAPTER 7

Enjoying Last Hurrahs Before Graduation

As a freshman, you probably felt like senior year was a lifetime away. There may even have been a few times along the way where you weren't sure you were going to make it to the end…but you did! And now, even though it feels like you were applying to college only yesterday, you're just a few steps away from graduation. In the midst of this mind-blowing revelation, the temptation to succumb to "senioritis" and coast through the rest of your time at college is all too real. Without a doubt, some goofing off is called for and well deserved. But there are still loose ends to tie up.

Use the insider tips in this chapter to put the cherry on top of your college experience. You'll discover last-hurrah ideas that include fully utilizing student resources and squeezing in a few more memorable moments. Remember your not-so-distant future can be positively or negatively affected by the decisions you make now, so make the most of these final months before you graduate!

Set Up an Informational Interview with Someone in Your Field

An informational interview is completely different than a job interview. Instead of a nerve-racking meeting where there's a job position at stake, you're having a less formal conversation with an employed professional. It's basically an opportunity to learn about what it's really like to work in a field that interests you.

You'll be able to ask the person any burning questions you may have, such as:

- How did you get into this field?

- What's a typical workday for you?

- What do you enjoy the most and least about your job?

- If you could start at the beginning of your career again, would you change your approach?

- What advice do you have for someone interested in a career in this field?

Informational interviews are invaluable for getting information about a company, job position, and/or general field. Prepare by brainstorming and even writing down the questions you want to ask ahead of time. Just don't go overboard: These meetings are typically fifteen to thirty minutes long.

Landing an informational interview might take some time as it's often a numbers game. Career services may be able to help, but expect to do most of the legwork on your own. Search online for tips on how to ask for one and where to seek out professionals to interview. And though it's not a job interview, it is in your best interest to look put together, so dress business casual (opt for dress pants or a skirt with a button-down top or blouse, and avoid anything dirty, wrinkled, baggy, or revealing). Informational interviews are a solid way to build career connections; do your best to make a good impression!

Secure an Internship Related to Your Major

Completing an internship related to your major is far superior to completing just any old internship. It will give you crucial real-life experience in your field and help set you apart from the rest of the new graduates. Additionally, if you perform well at your internship, they may offer you a full-time job in return.

The best time to apply for an internship is well in advance before you're set to graduate—as early as six months prior. The earlier you apply, the better your chances are for being selected. Of course, you can take an internship while in school, but an internship during the summer and/or after graduating is ideal because it's easier to handle when you don't have to juggle it with classes.

Find an internship by searching online job boards, networking, attending career fairs, or with the help of your school's career center. Internships are competitive, so don't get discouraged if you don't hear back about your application right away. If you're applying to ten or more every month, your persistence is sure to pay off! While you're waiting on responses, it's also a good idea to familiarize yourself online with how the typical internship works from start to finish.

Plan a Reunion-Style Dinner with Your Freshman Year Roomies

From freshman year to senior year, you've likely changed a lot as a person and so have your past roommates. It won't be long now until your graduating class scatters in the wind, so now is the perfect chance to reunite with the people you shared a dorm room or floor with during your first semester (or entire first year).

Reconnecting is sure to bring up fun memories (that may seem like they happened just yesterday—or an entire lifetime ago), along with feelings of nostalgia. You may be totally different people now, and that's okay: You still have shared experiences over which to reminisce. You'll get to say, "Remember that one time…?" maybe laugh about things that weren't so funny at the time, and enjoy a meal in good company.

Attend a Free Career Development Workshop

The career center (as well as a mix of clubs and organizations) at your school offers workshops that can help you land a job. They're free, so you have nothing to lose by going to at least one!

These workshops can teach you tons of different career-related skills. Workshop topics may include:

- Networking
- Job shadowing
- Making the best use of *LinkedIn*
- Alumni panels (where you get to ask past students about their job experiences)
- Dos and don'ts of interviewing
- Navigating a career fair
- Job-searching strategies

Any time you spend on preparing yourself for your future career is time well spent. Attending a free workshop (or two or three) can help ensure your transition to postgrad life goes smoothly. Armed with the right knowledge, you may be able to clear up some feelings of apprehension, zero in on which jobs to apply for, or even secure a job offer more quickly than your peers.

Turn the Constant Questions about Your Postgraduation Plans Into a Game

As soon as you become a senior, it's like the only thing people are interested in talking about with you are your postgraduation plans. You'll get to a point where all you want to do is let out a scream whenever you're asked, "How's the job search going?" Because, *hello*, hunting for work is usually not the most fun thing for anyone. Thanks for the reminder, Aunt Gloria!

While you can't stop the questions from coming, what you *can* do is have a little fun with it. Whenever someone fields you a "So, what are your plans after graduation?" instead of flipping the nearest table like a maniac who's finally snapped, you can provide a polite response and smile to yourself as you add a tally mark on your phone. Your friends will likely be pelted with the same questions themselves, so make a wager with them. Guess how many times each of you will be asked one of these questions before graduation day or who will be asked the most. This little game should be just enough of a distraction to keep you from spiraling into complete madness.

Update Your *LinkedIn* Profile with a Professional-Looking Headshot

Though your *LinkedIn* profile picture may seem inconsequential in the grand scheme of things, it can actually have an effect on your job search. Hiring managers are just as susceptible to bias (unconscious or not) as anyone else, and your profile picture is their first impression of you. So when you're trying to land your dream job, you will want to present yourself in the best light possible wherever potential employers may look.

Luckily, you don't need to hire a professional photographer to capture a quality headshot. You can enlist the help of a friend or do it yourself with your smartphone, a tripod, and a timer. If you do know someone with a DSLR camera, they might be willing to snap some photos of you for free or cheap. Be on the lookout for on-campus events (like career fairs) where you can get a pro headshot too!

In preparation for your mini photo shoot, consider how your outfit, posture, hair, and expression will come across. You may also want to look at examples online and read tips about how to optimize your profile picture. The right photo is beneficial not only for your profile, but it can be a nice little confidence boost too!

Get Letters of Recommendation

A strong letter of recommendation can be your golden ticket to graduate school, scholarships, and even your dream job. The best time to ask your professors for letters of recommendation is three to six weeks ahead of time, ideally as early as possible. College professors have a lot of students, which means they can quickly be swamped once requests start rolling in. By asking before everyone else starts asking, you can minimize your chance of getting something lackluster.

Professors with whom you've fostered a real relationship will be your best bet, as they can give more detailed, personalized recommendations. Meeting in person to make your request will further bolster your chances of receiving a glowing recommendation since they'll more easily be able to put a face to the name and you'll thus stand out among the sea of digital requests.

Once you get the green light, you'll want to follow up with an email that contains all the relevant information your professor needs to compose the letter. This will depend on what exactly you need a recommendation for, but you can find checklists and suggestions for materials to provide online. It also doesn't hurt to ask your professor what they need to write the best possible letter.

Finally, don't forget to thank your professors and keep them posted on how things turn out!

Chat about Grad School with a Professor or Advisor

Even if you aren't interested in attending straightaway, it's worthwhile to talk to a professor or advisor about graduate school. It's good to be aware of all your choices should you decide to continue your education at some point down the line. And if you've already set your sights on higher learning, it's *imperative* to get a jump on the process. There are a lot of due dates to keep track of and forms to submit. Grad school can be quite competitive; it's definitely the type of situation where the early bird gets the worm! Have a conversation with a professor or advisor to get guidance and valuable insights.

Savor Your Remaining Free Time

College can be a busy time in your life; however, entering the working world is a whole other ball game. There usually isn't a ton of time left over each day after working and commuting. And as much as your heart may yearn to be a happy little couch potato, a lot of the remaining time you have is spent on other responsibilities like making dinner and figuring out bills.

Take care to recognize and appreciate the free time you have now. Think about just how awesome it is to not have to be anywhere until 11 a.m. on a Tuesday when your first class starts. Or that you can stay out until 4 a.m. if you want and sleep in the next day. Your college years can be extraordinary; it's important to be thankful for all the little opportunities this experience affords you.

Take Your Last "First Day of School" Picture

As kids head off to school in the fall, #firstdayofschool pictures flood social media. Children of all ages pose with a smile and their backpack, or hold a sign announcing which grade they're about to start. Your parents probably took a photo of you on your first day of kindergarten (or maybe every first day through grade school) that's framed and on display, or tucked away in a scrapbook. Ask a friend to snap a picture of you on the first or last day of your senior year of college for a fun comparison and keepsake! You can get all dolled up or re-create that kindergarten pose and/or outfit.

Meet Five New People During Your Last Month

By now you probably have a well-established friend group that you love spending most of your time with. These are *your* people after all! But your opportunities to mingle and make new friends shrink considerably after you leave college. Take advantage of the remaining time you have left in this unique bubble and challenge yourself to branch out. The best friends are made in the most unexpected places, so get to know at least five new people before graduation. There's always room for one more bosom buddy in your life! Even if you don't strike up a friendship, any connections you form may prove helpful networking-wise later on.

Host an Ugly Sweater Contest

Make your final holiday season at college one to remember with a little friendly competition! There are two fun ways you can go about hosting an ugly sweater contest:

1. Create a flyer describing the event and send out invites a couple of weeks ahead of time. Guests will be on their own to find or create ugly sweaters and then will show up to the party already wearing them.

2. Or the contest can be more like a crafting event. You can pick up an assortment of sweaters at a discount store, provide glue guns, and ask each guest to bring a specific decorating supply (like glitter or pom-poms).

Either way, the goal is to have the tackiest, most over-the-top sweater. And the more the merrier, so invite friends, classmates, TAs, or whoever looks like they could use some holiday cheer. You can set out food, play games, sip on eggnog, and laugh at each other's outfits. Pick the winners with a group vote and give out prizes to the top three contenders. Fun prizes might be plastic trophies, a festive wine bottle sweater, or a coveted chocolate orange. It's sure to be a blast!

Visit All the Neighboring States

Take the opportunity to check out every state touching the one your college is in so you can say you've been to them at least once! You never know where you'll ultimately end up after graduation; it could be a while before you have the chance (if ever) again to visit these states. It's as good an excuse as any to squeeze in another road trip with friends too.

You could easily turn this activity into a mini adventure! Take a weekend to drive the entire perimeter of your college's state and hit up every neighboring one along the way. During your trip, you may discover cool tourist attractions, a state park you've never been to, delicious local food, or quiet, scenic roads while laughing too loud with your favorite people.

Hang Out with Your Friends As Much As Possible

Spend as much time and make as many new memories with your college friends as you can. Once you graduate who knows when you'll see them again face-to-face—or how often you will be able to get together once you are all busy with your professional lives. Change is an immutable part of life, and your friendships are just as sure to shift as the years pass.

Instead of worrying about how the future will unfold, cherish what you have now. Make 1 a.m. runs to your favorite fast-food joint, go to one more home game, goof around on campus, plan a special trip, and take joy in every moment you spend together.

Take an Alternative Spring Break

Make the most out of your senior year by skipping the typical costly spring break to volunteer either domestically or internationally instead. Alternative spring break (ASB) programs provide opportunities for students to travel while helping animals, people, or the environment at the same time. They usually offer ample time for leisure and adventure outside of the volunteer work as well, so it's the perfect way to do something meaningful while still having fun.

You may want to get involved with:

- Turtle nest monitoring and habitat protection in Galapagos

- Neighborhood revitalization in New Orleans

- Organic farming in Belize

- Temple renovation in Sri Lanka

- Elephant nursery work in Northern Thailand

- Coral reef conservation in Israel

- Teaching school children in Mexico

You can find a wide variety of ASB opportunities offered by organizations like Habitat for Humanity, Projects Abroad, GoEco, WWOOF, the American Hiking Society, or even your own college. A small financial contribution is normally required to cover housing, travel, and food, but the costs are more than reasonable, especially when considering it could be a once-in-a-lifetime trip. From immersing yourself in a culture different than your own to learning new skills, giving back, upgrading your resume, and exploring a foreign location, an ASB is sure to be a memorable adventure!

Spend an Entire Day Doing Nothing

It's easy to get caught up in the whirlwind of trying to make sure you accomplish every last thing you set out to do before the end of the school year. And if you've ever reached the bottom of an ice cream pint during a single sitting, you know that there *is* such a thing as too much of a good thing. Your heart's in the right place, but being on the go all the time can be taxing.

Never underestimate the amazingly restorative properties of a day where you have absolutely nothing on your plate. Make a point to spend an entire day doing nothing more than simply living in the moment. Take a nap, stay in your pajamas, order takeout, and make no provision to bask in the glory of a carefree, unplanned day. You may discover this is what you needed all along to let go of stress and recharge for whatever lies ahead.

Set a
School Record

While there are many ways you can leave your mark on campus, there's something weirdly wonderful about setting a school record. Organizing an event to break a regional, national, or world record is both challenging and wildly entertaining.

Some inspiring examples to get you started include:

- Rutgers University, 2009: Most "Where's Waldos" in one place
- Penn State, 2010: Longest distance traveled on a Slip 'N Slide in one hour
- Mississippi State, 2015: Most people ringing cowbells simultaneously

There's also the option to go for an individual stunt, like the Boise State and Bowdoin College students who set the respective records for longest time to balance a Hula-Hoop on their head while swimming and farthest grape toss and mouth catch.

No matter the outcome, your attempt will be one for the books. So go after the record for the world's largest cardboard box castle, game of Twister, water balloon fight, or something else entirely. Just aim to create a legacy you're proud to leave behind. And who knows, you could get your name in *Guinness World Records*.

Take a Selfie with All the Great People You've Met at College

Snap a picture with every one of your friends, along with anyone else who has had a positive effect on your time at college. This may include a few professors, your mentor, or a campus staff member you befriended.

You might feel silly asking for so many selfies (especially if you're not the selfie-taking type), but you'll be glad you did. Because even when your memories begin to fade you'll still have these pictures to recall your undergraduate years with joy. And during the times you're able to reconnect with your old college gang, you can share these treasures and revel in the nostalgia together.

Make an Over-the-Top Feast Using the Rest of Your Meal Points

Do what you have to do to squeeze every last drop out of your meal plan. If that means buying seven milkshakes, twelve bags of chips, and four bottled tea drinks, so be it. Unless your university is one of the few schools that will refund the unused portion of your meal plan, you're not getting that money back. Use it or lose it! Cash in your remaining meal points for an epic last feast of whatever looks good.

Decorate Your Graduation Cap in a Meaningful Way

Decorating your graduation cap is a fun way to express yourself and show off your personality in a sea of uniform gowns. Plus, your creative mortarboard can serve as a celebration of your achievements. You did it! And now you'll have a colorful memento of all of the work you put into your degree.

Your university may have guidelines for cap decorations (typically commonsense stuff like not using expletives). You should be able to find more information on the school website. But other than that, you can decorate your cap however you want.

From bows and jewels to major-related jokes and coordinated group decorations, there are limitless ways to get creative. Start by doing a quick online search for instant inspiration. You can also follow along with an online video. In the end, whatever decorations you choose should be meaningful to you, so follow your heart and see where it leads!

Say Goodbye to Your Favorite Professors

Graduating from college—and the buildup to it—is exciting. There are no more books to study or tests to take, and you're finally free to follow your passions in any way you see fit! However, at some point, you'll feel a twinge of sadness as the reality of it all sinks in. You may have cursed its existence from time to time, but this campus has become your home. There are parts of it that hold special meaning to you and people who you'll really miss.

Make sure you include the professors you have a personal connection with during your end-of-the-year hullabaloo, because they'll miss you too. And if there's anything you've been meaning to say, now is the perfect time! Whether the message is spoken in person or expressed with a handwritten card, your professors will really appreciate you taking the time to say thank you and goodbye.

Graduate Happy!

There's an absolutely *ridiculous* amount of things you can experience before you graduate college. From the first day of freshman year to the moment you walk across the stage to receive your diploma, you're the one calling the shots. All the choices you make are smaller elements of a greater whole.

However you end up spending your undergraduate years is up to you. You'll do a fine job so long as you keep your own personal satisfaction and happiness in mind at every step of the way. Don't wait until the very end to celebrate yourself and your achievements, or to reflect on and appreciate every great moment!

And remember: Life doesn't end after college. This is only the beginning of your journey.

Create Your Own Bucket List

- [ ] _____
- [ ] _____
- [ ] _____
- [ ] _____
- [ ] _____
- [ ] _____
- [ ] _____
- [ ] _____
- [ ] _____
- [ ] _____
- [ ] _____
- [ ] _____
- [ ] _____
- [ ] _____
- [ ] _____
- [ ] _____
- [ ] _____
- [ ] _____

- [ ] _____
- [ ] _____
- [ ] _____
- [ ] _____
- [ ] _____
- [ ] _____
- [ ] _____
- [ ] _____
- [ ] _____
- [ ] _____
- [ ] _____
- [ ] _____
- [ ] _____
- [ ] _____
- [ ] _____
- [ ] _____
- [ ] _____
- [ ] _____
- [ ] _____

INDEX

About the Author

Charlotte Lake is a Pacific Northwest transplant and writer for the popular site CollegeLifeMadeEasy.com. As a former broke college kid who's been there and done that, she specializes in helping students thrive more and stress less. When she's not writing, Charlotte enjoys sleeping in, bargain hunting, and fawning over old dogs.